VARIETY PACK

FIVE SHORT PLAYS

VARIETY PACK

FIVE SHORT PLAYS

E.M. SCHORB

HILL HOUSE   NEW YORK

ISBN: 979-8-218-55392-0

Cover Design: Selah Bunzey

for Patricia

and

with belated thanks to

*Dr. Saul C. Colin,
Erwin Piscator's Dramatic Workshop
School of the Theatre*

and

*Sanford Meisner,
The Neighborhood Playhouse*

INTRODUCTION

This is no theater of the absurd; on the contrary, it confronts us with everyday absurdities and perversities that seem to the public the most rational and normal. All five of these short plays present and press on us ethical conundrums, not to solve them but to dramatize and emphasize them as our own conundrums.

There is the elderly wealthy widow who, in the purest Cynic tradition so much alive in our time and place, cares only for herself and her poodle and not a bit for any other human being, attended by the young practical nurse who ends up by choking and killing the poodle and throwing it in the face of her patient. Here, as you see, it is not a struggle between good and evil, rather between two evils; the effect of the final violence is, anyhow, cathartic.

A bunch of secondary characters who are hilariously vulgar, graced with racist and sexist prejudices, like Aunt Myrtle and Uncle O'Toole in the first play, provide effective comic relief.

There's no comic relief in the penultimate play, whose only characters are a terrorist and a punisher. During the confrontation between them, the tied-up terrorist tries to justify himself saying that he was fighting against fascism, and the punisher replies: "You see, every baby is born a fascist. Every baby wants what it wants when it wants it. And this is as it should be. The thing is, you're like an infant. During the course of growing up, you never acquired a conscience."

Thomas Jefferson, whose political ideology of minimal government intervention was back in the early 19th century called liberal and now is called conservative—Jefferson our third president, is revived in the final play. The ethical conundrum here is about how to deal with the many substances to which humans may, and do, become addicted to the detriment of their health. What is to be done with alcohol, opium, or, more recently and fatally with fentanyl? The USA implemented Prohibition from alcohol for thirteen years, and this encouraged bootlegging and a plague of criminals like Al Capone. Later, Nixon's war against drugs filled USA jails to bursting with Blacks and Hispanics. Schorb's Jefferson cultivates cannabis in Monticello, enjoys his amontillado, and is unable to conceive of such future perversity.

The great merit of these five plays is, I think, that they help us perceive our present perversity.

Ricardo L. Nirenberg, Editor
Offcourse Literary Journal

HIRE ACTORS!

Being superficially
mourned would be a
last wicked joke on me.

Hire actors

who, though they have
never met me, can
read my story and
genuinely feel.

Hire actors

and be honest and
revile me at leisure
while the actors mourn.

Hire actors

who have been taught
the Method and know
their motivations.

Hire actors!

One good actor can feel
more than an average
family.

Hire actors!

E.M. Schorb
Dramatists Guild Quarterly

CONTENTS

AN ACTOR PREPARES

A Play in Five Scenes

Cast of Characters

Barry Hill: Aspiring actor, working
                     on docks, and superin-
                     tending artment house,
                     named The Van Gogh.

Maggie Hill: BARRY'S middle-aged
                     widowed mother.

Penny Rexham: BARRY'S somewhat
                     estranged girlfriend.

Aunt Myrtle: MAGGIE HILL'S sister.

Uncle O'Toole: MAGGIE HILL'S
                     brother-in-law, retired
                     leather worker.

Scene

Small Greenwich Village basement apartment,
lit by sidewalk-level windows. Kitchenette
stage left. Livingroom with usual furnishings.

Time

Mid-morning. Last Century.

2

<u>Scene 1</u>

SETTING: The HILL'S basement
apartment.

AT RISE: BARRY HILL, dressed in
jeans and shirt, stands,
stage right, talking into
land-line telephone
placed on a small table.

BARRY

Penny, I just can't do it, I tell you.
(*pause*)
I know, but you should have told them by now
that we weren't married, for Christ's sake!
(*pause*)
You could have made up anything—told them
I'd been drafted or deserted you. With them
on the West Coast, you could have told them I
left you flat and you needed that stipend again,
too.
(*pause*)
God! They must think I'm a rat, anyway, the
way I've always avoided meeting them. It
was O.K. when your old man was flying
Seattle to Tokyo, but now, Damn! He'll be
coming regularly to New York. I just can't

3

BARRY (*Cont'd*)

keep pretending to be your vanishing husband.
That's all there is to it!
    (*pause*)
All right. All right. But after this, you've <u>got</u>
to tell them . . . write them a letter, tell them
we got divorced. Mental cruelty or something.
Blame it on me. O.K. I'll come over and pick
you up first. Now leave me alone. I've got to
prepare for this <u>command</u> performance for
your parents. After a night on the docks I had
to bring in twenty cans for the Van Gogh. I
can't expect my mother to do that. She's
already cleaned the elevator. Now she's
working on our apartment. I'm exhausted.
This superintending a big apartment building
is wearing us both down to the nub.
    (*pause*)
O.K. —'bye now.

MAGGIE
    (*in kitchenette, having just overheard,*
    coming to face BARRY)
So when is this long-awaited meeting with her
parents going to take place, may I ask?

BARRY

Late today.

MAGGIE

Today! Oh, no. No! It can't be! Aunt Myrtle
and Uncle O'Toole are coming over from
Jersey this afternoon. I told you they were.
Don't you remember? I've got the place all
spick and span and a roast in the oven. You
have to be here and help me. We've got to
entertain them somehow. I want them to see
our new place here and how well we're getting
along, even though Dad's gone and left us
absolutely nothing. And that you're taking
good care of me. You've got to be here,
Barry!

BARRY

Oh, my God! A <u>second</u> command performance. It's like playing at two different
theatres at once. I'd forgotten. Don't worry.
I'll figure it out somehow. I'm noted for
doing ten things at once. Haven't you
noticed?

MAGGIE

*(entering kitchenette and returning
with two cups of coffee, offering
one to* BARRY*)*

I don't know how you ever got mixed up with
that girl, anyway. She smokes pot. She's a
skinny little Beatnik. She looks like a
Salvation Army poster in those clothes she

MAGGIE (*Cont'd*)
wears. And that Afro hair-do! An artist, my
ass! I don't know what you ever saw in her.

BARRY
(*sitting at a table, thoughtfully*)
You just don't know her, Mom. She's quick
and bright and has a wonderful skeptical view
of life and she's beautiful. She's more of a
friend than a girl friend, anyway. At least,
now. I don't think I'll be seeing much of her
anymore.

MAGGIE
For a while there, I thought you <u>were</u> going to
marry her. I know you were sleeping with her.

BARRY
That's none of your business.

MAGGIE
Since when is my son's sex life none of my
business, may I ask? You'll get a disease.

BARRY
Since your son says so, that's when! Besides,
I think there's someone else now. But I owe
Penny something. If I can't give her the real
thing, maybe I can act out a scene that'll be a

BARRY (*Cont'd*)
nice memory for her someday. I owe her that
much. I really do.
>   (*doorbell rings. BARRY goes to
>   speaker phone on wall to answer*)
What? Who's there?

UNCLE O'TOOLE
>   (*voice over speaker phone*)
Barry? That you? How do we find you?
We're in the lobby.

BARRY
>   (*to* MAGGIE, *hand over speaker*)
It's them! What're they doing here, so early?

MAGGIE
>   (*shrugs, alarmed, runs off*)
I have to spruce up. Quick!

BARRY
>   (*into speaker phone*)
Hi, yes, it's me. Just follow the stairway
down. I'll open the door for you.
>   (*steps over to open door* for
>   AUNT MYRTLE *and* UNCLE
>   O'TOOLE)

UNCLE O'TOOLE
Surprise! Surprise!

AUNT MYRTLE
(*through laughter*)
Here we are in Greenwich Village and I'm
ready for a gay day!

BARRY
Well, glad to see you. We weren't expecting
you so early, but great! <u>Great!</u>
(*hugs them both*)

UNCLE O'TOOLE
Say, this is a pretty fancy building.

AUNT MYRTLE
What a lovely apartment!

UNCLE O'TOOLE
Do you mean you get this apartment free? Do
you get tips, Barry? Well, let <u>me</u> give you a
tip. Save your money. Ha—ha-ha!

AUNT MYRTLE
(*looking around room*)
What lovely curtains!

UNCLE O'TOOLE
What smells so good?

MAGGIE
(*Enters, having changed and
made-up*)
Hello, you two! Oh, I'm glad to see you!
(*hugs and kisses them.*)
Sit down, sit down. Relax.
(*goes to sideboard, begins
preparing drinks.*)

AUNT MYRTLE
Maggie, you look lovely!

UNCLE O'TOOLE.
You're lookin' good, Barry, lost a little
weight?

AUNT MYRTLE
Do you get a salary here, too?

MAGGIE
(*smiling, offering drinks*)
Not too early, is it?

UNCLE O'TOOLE
Never too early for cheers! Quite a deal
you've got here. Sláinte!
(*raises glass and ALL join*)

(END OF SCENE)

<u>Scene 2</u>

SETTING: Stage right, NYC subway platform. Stage left, dark.

AT RISE: BARRY and PENNY enter breathlessly, then stand, waiting for train. They both wear suits. BARRY caries large plastic bag bearing store logo. PENNY carries a native-American beaded bag.

PENNY
(after gaining composure and fixing her hair which has come loose a bit, turning to BARRY)
Well, how do I look?

BARRY
You look really nice, Penny. Like a beautiful black girl in search of her God. I haven't seen you so dressed up since . . . since I don't know when. Here, let me—
(steps close to her, pats her hair, steps back, looking more closely at her face)

BARRY (*Cont'd*)
you've got two red spots on your cheeks. Let
me tone you down a bit.
>   (*takes out handkerchief, dabs
>   her cheeks*)

You went a little too heavy on the Max Factor,
I think. I've been taking a course in theatrical
makeup, you know.

PENNY

You know I never use this stuff. The only
stuff I paint is on canvas! Oh, this is such a lot
of bullshit. If only I didn't have to pretend
with them.

BARRY

My sentiments exactly!

PENNY

To hell with it! Come on; let's go!

BARRY

Well, you don't want to look like you're ready
for a war dance. You're not high on pot, are
you? Wait a minute. Turn around. You've
got cat hairs all over your skirt. After all, we
<u>are</u> going to the Plaza.
>   (*brushes her skirt, trying to
>   remove cat hair while turning her
>   all around*)

PENNY

What's in the bag?

BARRY

I brought you something. I knew you'd be
dragging that beaded Indian purse with you. It
looks like something you picked out of an
ashcan soomewhere in New Mexico. Here's a
nice pocketbook I just bought for you.
   (*pulls black patent pocketbook from*
   his plastic bag, hands to her)

PENNY

Oh, bullshit! Now what'll I do with the old
one?

BARRY

Just put it inside the new one.

PENNY

Barry, this thing is way too big! Oh, to hell
with it! Train's coming. Let's go! It's all just
a lot of bullshit!
   (*Stage* RIGHT *darkens. Stage*
   LEFT *light rises in* PENNY'S
   apartment.)

(END OF SCENE)

<u>Scene 3</u>

SETTING: PENNY'S apartment,
                  walls painted psychedelic
                  designs, mattress on floor,
                  books scattered, easel with
                  large half-done portrait of
                  BARRY as Hamlet canvass,
                  general mess.

AT RISE: BARRY and PENNY enter.

BARRY

Aaahhh. What a performance! I feel like such
a liar.

PENNY
*(kicking off shoes and pulling off
her jacket, skirt, blouse and
wriggling into dungarees)*
It's a bullshit world, Barry.

BARRY
(looking around)
Why won't you clean this place up? For that
matter, why don't <u>you</u> dress up once in a
while. You looked so lovely today.

PENNY

I don't belong to the bullshit world, Barry.
You're crazy, you know. You'll kill yourself—trying to run that apartment building,
working on the docks, keeping up your classes
at the Dramatic Workshop . . . and taking care
of your bitching mother. You'll kill yourself.
            (*sits down on mattress and pulls
        BARRY *down beside her*)
And now you've got a girlfriend at the
dramatic school. I know you do. It's all
bullshit!

BARRY

            (*holding his head in his hands*)
This place is full of fleas—from that cat. I can
see them jumping around.

PENNY

It's not fleas—it's Champagne things you're
seeing—thanks to my father. But, oh Barry,
wasn't it really nice? They're real squares, but
aren't they nice? Do you like them, Barry?

BARRY

It was, and they were, and yes, I do. I was
impressed by the fact that your Dad had been a
fighter pilot. Did you know I played one
once? And they didn't seem to mind that

BARRY (*Cont'd*)

you're married to an ofay actor, who only
<u>played</u> a fighter pilot.

PENNY

My dad looked so handsome in his uniform.
And Mom is still beautiful. And they really
<u>loved</u> you! And they thought you were funny.

BARRY

And your mom looked like you, just older.
Your dad was handsome as Sidney Poitier and
she was beautiful and they seemed to like me
even though I <u>was</u> a white dude, and a fake
and a phoney.

PENNY

What do you mean, a phoney? I knew you
were pretending for them today. I knew you
were. I know you're getting ready to leave
me, too. I always knew you would, in the end.
You're becoming part of the bullshit world.
> (*begins to cry, wipes her eyes
> with shirt tail.*)

Oh, Barry, it would be so wonderful if we
could just stay together.
> (*gets up, goes to table, picks up
> and takes a drag on a pot pipe,
> looks at* BARRY, *inspired*)

Want a drag?

BARRY

Not right now. I'm already seeing fleas.

PENNY

Don't you really and truly love me a little?

BARRY

That's the hell of it, Penny. I _do_ love you.
I'm tied to you. I feel responsible for you.
Right now I'd like to stay with you, you and
your nutty cat and your fleas, but right now,
I've got to go. I've got a house full of aunts
and uncles I've gotta tend to. I promised
Mom. Remember, I was on the docks all
night. I haven't had any sleep. I've got to go.
> (*Gets up.* PENNY *throws herself
> into* BARRY's *arms*. He stands,
> patting her back.)

PENNY

It's a bullshit world.

(END OF SCENE)

<u>Scene 4</u>

<u>SETTING:</u>   The HILL'S basement apartment. The next morning.

<u>AT RISE:</u>   UNCLE O'TOOLE and AUNT MRYTLE enter living room in nightclothes. MAGGIE rises, from couch in blanket and nightclothes. BARRY, dressed, in kitchenette making coffee.

UNCLE O'TOOLE
(*sprightly, full of energy*)
Wow! That was some night, Barry. I could've kept on going. Glad you got back to take us around and showing us that place— what was it called? Your Father's Mustache? That banjo music reminded me of the old days.

(MAGGIE si*ts back down on couch, hung-over, holding her head.*)

17

AUNT MYRTLE
(*groggy, taking coffee from*
BARRY *and sitting down*
at table)
Oooh, Barry, it <u>was</u> fun, but I still can't figure
out why you and Maggie want to live over
here in this den of iniquity. Seems like a
funny place, to me. Is there much of that
'mess-sin-ation' going on around here?

BARRY
(*startled by her question*)
Too early for that, Aunt Myrtle, but about as
much as anywhere, I guess.

UNCLE O'TOOLE
I don't approve of that; do you, Barry?

BARRY
I've got nothing against it. I wouldn't go out
of my way to marry a black woman, but if I
fell in love with a black woman, and we
wanted to marry each other, I'd marry her.

UNCLE O'TOOLE
(*shocked*)
You <u>would!</u> But suppose you had a daughter,
you wouldn't want your daughter to marry
one, would you?

BARRY

Well, it looks like if I had already married one,
and I had a daughter, I couldn't offer much of
an objection to my daughter marrying one,
too, could I?

UNCLE O'TOOLE
(*thoughtfully*)
Mmmm. I take your point.

AUNT MYRTLE
(*alarmed*)
You're not going to marry one, are you,
Barry?

BARRY

I haven't been asked.

AUNT MYRTLE

My God, Maggie, Barry isn't thinking of
marrying a colored girl, is he?

MAGGIE

He's only teasing you. Wake up.

UNCLE O'TOOLE
(*laughing*)
Oh, I get it.

AUNT MYRTLE

Well, for a minute there, I thought my poor
sister was going to become the grandmother of
a pickaninny. And me the great-aunt of one.
You mustn't do that to her, to us, Barry. I
know you've got some weird ideas, but she's
had a hard enough life as it was, with your
father.
            (*inspired*)
Oh, what a strange man your father was! I
wouldn't have put it past <u>him</u> to marry a
colored girl. He was a drunkard!

MAGGIE

Now let's leave him out of this. He's dead
and buried and I'm just trying to wake up.
He's gone to his rest. Let's not talk about him
when he's not here to defend himself.

AUNT MYRTLE

Drank himself to death. I was thinking of the
life he led <u>you</u>—called you a Negative Force
all the time just because you wanted him to get
a job. My dear Albert has never treated me in
such a way. He's worked hard all his life. He
always supported his wife and children; didn't
you dear?

UNCLE O'TOOLE
Yeah, but sometimes I think maybe old Barry
Senior had the right idea.

AUNT MYRTLE
Hush! Well, it was a terrific night, Barry.
Thanks for taking us out and showing us the
sights, but I was wondering . . . remember that
man at the bar we saw somewhere?
Remember? Wonder why he wore his hair
like that?

UNCLE O'TOOLE
He looked like a girl, to me. And not a very
pretty one.

AUNT MYRTLE
He did, did he? You aren't becoming a
Villager, are you? One evening doesn't
change a man does it, Maggie?

UNCLE O'TOOLE
Hey, I'm a tough leather worker from Joisey.
Look at these knuckles!

AUNT MYRTLE
Maybe you were once, but now you're an old
fart. But you're my old fart and I love you.
            (*to* BARRY)

AUNT MYRTLE (*Cont'd*)
But, what I want to know is, why do you live
over here, anyway?

UNCLE O'TOOLE
Was he queer?

AUNT MYRTLE
I'd still like to see a lesbian.

UNCLE O'TOOLE
(*trying to remember*)
What was that bar you took us to, Barry?

BARRY
Oh, the White Horse Tavern. That was where
Dylan Thomas drank himself to death.
Remember that picture of him on the wall?
The place is nearly a shrine to him.

AUNT MYRTLE
As far as I could see, it was just a dump. And
who was this Dylan Thomas and where did he
get such a funny name, anyway?

BARRY
He was a famous Welsh poet.

UNCLE O'TOOLE
Famous for getting drunk and not supporting

UNCLE O'TOOLE (*Cont'd*)
his wife and children. I heard all about the
bum.

AUNT MYRTLE (*proudly*)
Your Uncle O'Toole knows just about every-
thing. Go ahead, ask him about something.
Ask him!

MAGGIE
I've got something to ask him, and you, too,
Myrtle. And think about it before you answer.
You know, this superintending job isn't as
easy as it sounds. Barry's going to school and
working nights on the docks and keeping this
whole building going all the time. He doesn't
have much time left over for me. And you
both keep asking us why we're living over
here. I've been thinking . . .

UNCLE O'TOOLE
Yeah. I've been sizing up what the upkeep on
a building like this might be. Lottsa work, I
can tell.

AUNT MYRTLE
Maggie, why don't you come back to Jersey
with us? We'd love to have you. We've got
that spare room we can let you have . . . or rent
. . . and Barry, well, he's a strong young man.

AUNT MYRTLE (*Cont'd*)
He can take care of himself. He can come
over sometimes to see you. And us, of course.
What would you think of that?

UNCLE O'TOOLE
Yes, Maggie, do. You'd like being back in
Jersey. And you wouldn't have to be at the
beck and call of all these snooty tenants. I bet
they keep you both jumping.

BARRY
(*to* MAGGIE)
Can't say I'm too surprised to hear you say
that, Mom. Have you all been planning this?
I can't keep the building without a woman. Is
that the reason you're here? Did you plan
this? Are you going to leave me in the lurch?
I won't mind, if you want to. I can settle up
with the management.

MAGGIE
I'm too old to run this big house. I know you
haven't had a day off and I know you're tired.
I don't like the folks in this building. And the
neighborhood's . . . well, it's not like Jersey,
where I know people, where I grew up. You
know, where it's familiar to me. It's weird
here, that's all! All these weirdos. I know you
like them Barry, but they're not for me.

BARRY

I'm exhausted. I think this is a good idea.
Mom, we can't make it together. I've tried to
help you, but you'd be better off with them.
Let's give up the Van Gogh.

UNCLE O'TOOLE

He cut his ear off! For a prostitute!

AUNT MYRTLE

Was she a lesbian? Well, nevermind. Let's
do it. We'll help you pack your things and the
three of us'll go back today. There's plenty of
room in the car. That is, if the cops haven't
towed us away for being parked in a no
parking space. We'll go this very afternoon!

UNCLE O'TOOLE

Then it's settled. Are we all agreed?

ALL
(lifting coffee cups in toast)
Yes! Settled! Agreed!

(END OF SCENE)

<u>Scene 5</u>

SETTING: PENNY'S apartment.
                  Same as before.

AT RISE: BARRY enters, suitcase
                  behind his back.

BARRY
(calling, setting suitcase in corner)
Penny. Oh, Penny!)

PENNY *(enters)*
Barry! I didn't expect to see <u>you</u> today. Your
Aunt and Uncle gone?

BARRY
Yeah. This afternoon.

PENNY
How'd it go, last night?

BARRY
I took them everywhere. I'm exhausted and
hung-over as hell. We spent a couple of hours
at Your Father's Mustache, you know, great
pitchers of beer and Gay Nineties banjo music.
Then we hit—must have been twenty bars—
and ended up at the White Horse, where Uncle

BARRY (*Cont'd*)
O'Toole simply astounded me with his dumb-
founding knowledge of modern literature by
saying he knew all about Dylan Thomas.

PENNY
(*laughing*)
See, you never know about these folks from
the sticks.

BARRY
And Aunt Myrtle. All she could think about
was wanting to see some <u>lesbians.</u> I can't
imagine exactly what she had in mind, but I
think she left somewhat disappointed. But
they had a great time and thanked me for it.
You know me, being an actor, I like to be
liked—even though I had to spend every last
cent I had on them.

PENNY
You gave them a good time, Barry. That's
what counts.

BARRY
I wanted to give you and your parents a good
time yesterday, too. At the beginning I looked
at that day as a big challenge, an acting
challenge. And, acting <u>is</u> lying of sorts—well

BARRY (*Cont'd*)

pretending—but, as I learned, it was lying to
tell a greater truth. At the hotel, with your
parents, I was very attentive to you, you know.
I wanted to show them that I loved you,
which, in fact . . . I believe I do.

PENNY

You don't have to say that to me. I know all
about that girl at the Dramatic Workshop.

BARRY

That's only acting, Penny. This is the real
thing. Yesterday, at the hotel I thought the
whole thing was not only preposterous,
because we were lying to your folks, but sad,
too. Sad because then I thought I wouldn't be
with you much longer, and it seemed almost a
crime to commit so near the end of our time
together. I played the Hairy Ape once, you
know, and yesterday, for a while, I felt a
certain nostalgia for the part. But I was
getting somewhere—it was that thing that I
was learning—lying to tell a greater truth. I
didn't quite know it then. But I know it now.
Stanislavski! I do love you, Penny.

PENNY

You mean it isn't all just a lie, an act, for my
folks?

BARRY

No, no, no, my nutty little misanthrope. I'm
gonna move in with you, if you'll have me.
See?

   (*points to suitcase in corner.*
   kisses her.)

PENNY

Oh, Barry! You know you really snowed
them yesterday, with all your charm. They
think you're the best thing that ever happened
to me. And so do I, Barry Hill. So do I.

BARRY

And I know the difference between acting and
lying now, too, my love.

(CURTAIN)

THE PRACTICAL NURSE

Cast of Characters

<u>Cora Freemantle</u>:   An elderly wealthy widow.

<u>Lorna Chandler</u>:   A young practical nurse.

Scene

Cora Freemantle's home in a Southern city.
The house is separated by a yard from houses
on either side. The action takes place in Mrs.
Freemantle's bedroom, around the hospital
bed she has had installed.

Time

Spring, 1977.

SETTING: Cora Freemantle's
                  bedroom.

AT RISE: Late morning. CORA
                  has been napping. She
                  wakes as LORNA enters.

                  LORNA
          (*steps into bedroom*)
I'm Lorna Chandler. Your son sent me.

                  CORA
The nurse. Did you lock the door behind you?
I didn't like waiting here with the door
unlocked. There's a bad element, you know. I
don't know why that son of mine has to do
things in such an . . . unorthodox manner.

                  LORNA
I locked the door.

                  CORA
Yes. Good. What did you say your . . .

                  LORNA
Lorna Chandler.

CORA

Yes. Lorna. Do you mind?

LORNA

No, I don't mind. May I call you Cora?

CORA

Well . . . . Yes, of course. You are a registered nurse?

LORNA

A practical nurse.

CORA

Isn't that . . . I mean—you don't have a degree or anything.

LORNA

I have passed all the necessary examinations.

CORA

But you are quite young. I should think you would be in a good nursing school—something to advance yourself.

LORNA

Money.

CORA

Ah, yes, I see. Money. Well, perhaps in

34

CORA (*Cont'd*)
future. . . In any case, did my son explain my
difficulties?

LORNA
He said you had a bad heart.

CORA
No, no. That's true, but I can get around ordinarily. But I got dizzy with the high blood-
pressure and I fell. Or perhaps I twisted my
ankle. But I fell. But the fall wasn't it. The
ankle was it. I mean—I can't get about. I
can't put any weight at all on the ankle. The
pain is excruciating.

LORNA
What did the doctor . . .

CORA
Sprained ankle. Stay off it. See the support?
(*She pulls the covers back to
display her bandaged leg.*)
Ordinarily, bad heart and all, I can get around.
I walk my dog, Suzy Wong. By the way,
where is Suzy? I didn't hear her bark when
you came in. She always barks. You didn't
let her out when you came in, did you?

LORNA

She barked. I guess you were dozing. She's
fine, now. Sleeping.

CORA

With her paws under her chin. Yes, I must
have been dozing. You're sure you locked the
door?

LORNA

I locked it. You have a lovely home.

CORA

Yes, I think so. Now, you understand that you
are to stay with me for the weekend, prepare
and serve my meals, help me to the bath-
room—well, you understand what I require?
My son told you?

LORNA

Yes, he told me.

CORA

Sit down, won't you. You make me nervous
just standing there.

LORNA

I'm sorry.
            (*She sits down near bed.*)

CORA

You have things? A suitcase?

LORNA

I left them in the living room.

CORA

Well, there's a guest room upstairs. The maid
uses it. She's black. You don't mind that do
you?

LORNA

Of course not.

CORA

Well, not necessarily "of course not," but
good; you take that. This is not a very big
house.

LORNA

But very nice.

CORA

Yes, I think so. I don't need a big house and I
won't waste money.

LORNA

No.

CORA

My second husband left me this house. When
he died.

LORNA

Yes.

CORA

Do you want some coffee or something?

LORNA

No.

CORA

Where's your coat?

LORNA

Outside, on my suitcase.

CORA

Well, why don't you see to your things. Take
them up to your room. Get settled. Then come
back down and make some coffee. I'd like
some.

LORNA

You'd like some?

CORA

Yes, I would. After just waking up. What
time is it, anyway?
(*They check their watches.*)

LORNA

Nearly noon, Friday.

CORA

(*eying* LORNA *with interest*)
Yes. My son was here this morning. I dozed,
and here you are—Lorna. Chandler—that
name rings a bell. That's an old family.

LORNA

Yes, an old family.

CORA

Yes, I recall. Substance. Are you a cousin?
Oh, forgive me, dear. I didn't mean—

LORNA

Distant. Yes, a distant cousin.

CORA

No offense. An old lady gets used to speaking
her mind. We get tactless, I'm afraid.
(*She holds up her wristwatch.*)

39

CORA (*Cont'd*)
Compensates for losing our other faculties.
Can't see too well—can't walk—etc.—but at
least you can say what you think.

LORNA
Yes, that's good. Say what you think.

CORA
(*her good humor dampened*)
Yes. Well, why don't you go on and put your
things away.

LORNA
Yes. Up in the black maid's room.

CORA (*annoyed*)
Yes, at the head of the stairs.

LORNA
Yes. And then you want some coffee.

CORA
I'd like coffee—yes.

LORNA
Very well.

CORA

Very well? You sound like an English butler
in an old movie.

LORNA

I'm sorry. I'll go now.
          (*rises and leaves CORA looking after*)

CORA

          (*hesitates, then draws her bedside
          phone to her and dials*)
Oh, I'm so glad I caught you, Iris. It's about
this nurse your husband has sent over here to
take care of me—what? What do you mean,
you have to run, Mother Freemantle? I'm
talking to you. And why do you, after fifteen
years of marriage to my son, insist on calling
me "Mother Freemantle?" My name is Cora.
What? Wait a minute, I want to speak to you.
I don't care about the children—
          (CORA *becomes aware of* LORNA'S
          presence. Looks up to see LORNA
          *standing in the doorway, now wearing
          a white uniform.*)
Oh, never mind, Iris. Iris? Iris?
          (*To* LORNA)
She hung up. My own daughter-in-law hung
up on me. Rude! Rude! Rude!
          (*She bangs down the receiver.*)
What is it, Lorna? Where's my coffee?

LORNA

Would you like anything with your coffee?

CORA

What?

LORNA

Perhaps a little wine?

CORA

Wine? What <u>are</u> you talking about? Coffee,
that's all. Just coffee. I don't drink.

LORNA

Oh. Because there's wine in the kitchen.
Several bottles of wine.

CORA

It must be the maid's.

LORNA

Oh. She has very good taste. Very expensive.
You must pay her well.

CORA

What business is that of yours? I pay her what
maids get.

LORNA

Black maids? Black domestics?

CORA (*pauses*)

Yes. I don't know where she gets the wine.
Oh, bother, of course it's my wine. I have a
right to have wine if I want it, don't I? This is
my house, isn't it? What am I sparring with
you about?

LORNA

I'm your nurse, Mrs. Freemantle. You have
high blood pressure. You should not drink
wine. You were drinking wine when you
became faint, and that led to your sprained
ankle. I am merely trying to do my job.

CORA

Of course. But I will have my wine if I wish
it, doctors, nurses or no. In fact—

LORNA

A glass with your coffee—?

CORA

No coffee. A glass of wine.

LORNA

As you wish.

CORA

There you go again—Lorna—sounding like an
English butler. Are you deliberately trying to
make me uncomfortable in my own house?

                    LORNA
No, Mrs. Freemantle.

                    CORA (*exasperated*)
Cora! Cora! My name is Cora!

                    LORNA
Yes—Cora.

                    CORA
You are trying to make me see that I should
not have the wine, is that it?

                    LORNA
I'll get it.

                    CORA
Don't ignore me!

                    LORNA (*standing*)
No.

                    CORA
Bother! Go on, then!
          (CORA *fidgets in irritation while*
          LORNA *goes to kitchen and returns*
          almost immediately with two glasses of
          red wine on a silver tray.)
What is that? Are you having a glass of wine,
too? Aren't you on duty, or something?

LORNA

I didn't think you'd like to drink alone.

CORA (*sarcastically*)

That was thoughtful of you, I must say.
        (*She sips her wine.*)
Is Suzy Wong still sleeping?

LORNA

Yes, I think so.

CORA

(*to make conversation*)
She's a Pekinese, you know. No mixed blood.
Highly nervous. That's why I was surprised
that I didn't hear her barking when you came
in. You must get on with dogs.

LORNA

I don't care for them.

CORA

How can you say that? Everyone likes dogs.

LORNA

Not everyone. When I was a little girl, I was
walking with my mother and father—walking
ahead of them and somewhat behind a stray
dog who, for no reason that I have ever been
able to discover, turned around suddenly and

LORNA (*Cont'd*)

mauled me. He bit my hand—there, you can
still see the teeth marks. The little ones bark
and the big ones bite—like people.

CORA

It's very unfair of you to base your opinion of
dogs on an isolated incident.

LORNA

It wasn't isolated to me. I was five and it was
my hand.

CORA

That doesn't make sense.

LORNA

It does to me.

CORA

It's a perverse attitude.

LORNA

But I guess we are all perverse, each in his
own way. The word means nothing.

CORA

I know what perverse means. I was a school
teacher.

LORNA

That must have been many years ago, in better times. Were there better times?

CORA

Yes, I think so. I think those were better times in some ways. But these are <u>my</u> better times.

LORNA

You mean because you have money now.

CORA

Yes. Money and security. But you weren't alive during the Depression. You wouldn't know.

LORNA

Then why do you say they were better times?

CORA

Not the Depression. I meant the times before, the Twenties. When I was young and starting out. They were better times—for the world. But these are my better times.

LORNA

You married wealthy men.

CORA

(*looks at her to see if she intends
any insult; decides not*)
Yes. During the Depression, when I saw what
could be, I decided to marry well, if I could.

LORNA

And you could, because you were good-
looking and knew it.

CORA

Yes, I think so. Yes. And I did. I married
well, and—

LORNA

And now you are a wealthy woman. You have
a black domestic and a practical nurse and, if
you wanted, you could have more.

CORA

I don't like to waste money. I don't need
more than I have.

LORNA

You have it just as you want it.

CORA

Yes, I think so.

LORNA

But you don't care for your children.

CORA

Of course I do. What made you think that?

LORNA

Because you didn't marry for love. You
married for money.

CORA

I didn't say that I didn't marry for love.

LORNA

But you suggested it.

CORA

Give me a cigarette.

LORNA
(*supplying a cigarette and a light*)
You shouldn't smoke, you know.

CORA
(*puffing to get light*)
Good. Now that you've said that, I hope
you'll allow me to enjoy this in peace.

LORNA

Of course.

CORA

No, I don't care much for my children. You
have insight, I'll say that for you.

LORNA

And less for your grandchildren.

CORA

I can't stand the little demons.

LORNA

I could tell by the way you referred to them
when you were talking to your daughter-in-
law. I didn't mean to overhear—

CORA

But you did. In fact, I was trying to get-ahold
of my son to ask him about you.

LORNA

Oh. Why?

CORA

Because you seemed—distracted, I guess is
the word—I wanted to know something about
you.

LORNA

But he wouldn't know anything about me. I

LORNA (*Cont'd*)

come from an agency. You'd have to call them.

CORA

What agency?

LORNA

Guess.

CORA

Guess? What are you talking about?

LORNA

No, I mean you'd never guess.

CORA

I'm not in the habit of playing guessing games, young lady.

LORNA

The Nightingale Nursing Service.

CORA

Oh.

LORNA

Yes, isn't it cute? Do you want to call them?

CORA

Of course not. I was just curious. Old women
are curious, you know.

LORNA

Yes, I know.

CORA

You know, Lorna, there's something in the
way you speak—I can't put my finger on it—

LORNA

I'm sorry. I'm doing my best to make conversation, to keep you company.

CORA
(*shaking her head*)
No, no. I'm sorry, dear. Just an old woman's
frustration at not being able to do for herself.
Will you get me another glass of wine, dear?

LORNA

You shouldn't have another, should you?

CORA

I suppose not, but—

LORNA

But you want one anyway.

CORA

Yes.

LORNA

You want what you want when you want it.

CORA

(*rising irritation*)
Yes. Don't be impertinent. But yes, I want
what I want when I want it—and I pay a good
deal to have it that way.

LORNA

You know, Mrs. Freemantle—Cora—you
remind me of my mother.

CORA

I suppose that's a compliment.

LORNA

Well, in a way. I envy people who can just
shut everything else out but what they want,
themselves. It's godlike.

CORA

I'm not sure I understand.

LORNA

Let me get your wine.
(*leaves room and returns with wine*)

53

CORA

What did you mean by—

LORNA

Oh, I don't know what I'm talking about, I
admit it. Most people don't, but I do, sometimes. Tell me about your first husband, girl
to girl.

CORA (shrugs)

There's not much to tell.

LORNA

But you had children by him.

CORA

Yes, that's true. Two. A boy—my son,
Jacob—and a daughter, Carol.

LORNA

Where's your daughter?

CORA

She lives in California, thank God! I've cut
her out for leaving me—old and ill. Jacob is
the only one I can count on. Besides, she has
twins.

LORNA

You don't care for them?

54

CORA

The truth is, I don't care for children.

LORNA

They have to be tended, watched over, looked
after, and loved.

CORA

They're a nuisance.

LORNA

They steal your thunder.

CORA

I don't know what that means.

LORNA

Children must come first.

CORA

That's a strange attitude for a young woman.

LORNA

No, not at all. <u>Yours</u> is strange to me.

CORA

There's nothing strange about it. What do you
know about children? I've had them, and
grandchildren.

                    LORNA
I almost had one.

                    CORA
Almost?

                    LORNA
When I was sixteen. My mother made me
have an abortion. I wasn't married. The boy
was gone. Not at all an unusual story.

                    CORA
Your mother did the right thing.

                    LORNA
Why do you think that? She never loved me.
She loved herself. Now I would have had a
child to love.

                    CORA
You would have been alone in the world with
a child to support. You're young, now, and
free. You can have another child when you
wish.

                    LORNA
How can you say that? Another child! As if
children were interchangeable, like pet dogs,
to be replaced!

CORA

Oh, but you can't replace a dog. Dogs are—
almost human.

LORNA

Humans _are_ human!

CORA

Now, now. I understand how you feel, but—

LORNA

But you obviously don't understand how I
feel, anymore than my mother did.

CORA

Well. Well, now, calm yourself. I'm the
patient here. You should be taking care of me.

LORNA
                    (_losing control_)
You! You! How can you think of nothing
else but yourself? You're a selfish old
woman, don't you know that? Don't you
realize what you are?
                    (_Shocked_, CORA _struggles to rise._
                    LORNA _advances toward the bed,_
                    pushes CORA _back._)
Don't try to get up. You'll fall, and it'll be my
fault for letting you. You wouldn't take the
blame yourself, would you?

CORA

Are you crazy, young woman? What are you
trying to do?

LORNA

Just take care of you and your hateful little
peke.

CORA

Suzy? Where is Suzy? What have you done
with my Suzy?

LORNA

I'll get her for you. You'd like to have her in
bed with you, wouldn't you?

CORA (*whimpering*)
Yes. Please get me Suzy. Please bring me my
little Suzy Wong.

LORNA
(*Leaves room and returns, holding limp
dog from its leash, dangling, lifeless.
She swings dog onto bed.*)
Here!

CORA
(*screams*)

LORNA

She must have got tangled in the leash. Poor
dear. But you can keep her in bed with you, if
you wish.

CORA (*breathless*)

Help . . . I can't . . .
(*She gasps for air, falls back on
pillows, silent.*)

LORNA
(*watching* CORA, *picking up phone
and dialing*)
There's plenty of time. Hello? Come over
now and pick up Suzy Wong. Yes, Iris,
everything is fine. Before I call emergency, I
want this damned little dead beast in your
care, where I hope it won't take you very long
to discover that it's had such a coochie-coo
sad accident. Tell Jake everything went as
planned. And, Iris, I warn you, don't either of
you forget for one minute that this house is
<u>mine</u>!
(*slams down phone*)

(CURTAIN)

WAITING FOR GRACE

Cast of Characters

<u>Tod Mitchell</u>:	A writer, about thirty.
<u>Grace Mitchell</u>:	TOD's wife, in her mid-twenties.
<u>Spring Mitchell</u>:	TOD'S mother, in her mid-sixties.
<u>"Butsy" Suddeth</u>:	A middle-aged caddy.
<u>Jean Shaw</u>:	A teacher-social worker in her twenties.
<u>Sophia Bennett</u>:	A Welsh woman in her late seventies, a former actress, and a poet.
<u>Delivery Boy</u>:	Young boy.

Scene

A large, bright room serving as both living room and dining room of a rear apartment on the "parlor" floor of a Brooklyn brownstone. Across the rear from left to right: a door that opens to a hall and the street; a kitchen area, with a refrigerator partially hidden by a large

screen; and a short bookcase with a record
player on top. Stage left, down from door: a
table with a lamp; a couch, end to audience;
and a small desk on which sits a lamp,
typewriter and a telephone. The room is
cheerfully, tastefully, but inexpensively
decorated. Prints by modern painters are hung
about. There are several house plants. The
floors are polished parquetry. There is a
bright oval throw rug in front of the couch.

<u>Time</u>

Ten o'clock Saturday morning. The 1960s.

ACT I

SETTING: At center, facing the audience, TOD MITCHELL sits at a large dining room table, drinking from a mug of beer. He has shaved and showered. He is neatly combed, dressed and pressed, but has a decidedly "artistic" appearance. His mother, SPRING MITCHELL, sits to his right. She is a pretty woman who looks fifteen years younger than her age. At his left sits BUTSY SUDDETH, a short, red-headed, ruggedly handsome man. SPRING is drinking beer, BUTSY a whiskey and soda.

AT RISE: They are talking cheerfully.

SPRING

I can't believe it! It's just wonderful!

TOD

You see, I got up about nine with a terrific bloody hangover, and I was just having a beer—trying to get my head together—when

TOD (*Cont'd*)

the phone rang. Well, when I heard the voice
the thought flashed through my mind: What's
Jerry—(*To* BUTSY) that's my agent—what's
Jerry doing calling me on a Saturday morning?
I was still in a fog. "Well," he says, "I've sold
your novel." I said: "What?" I didn't think
I'd heard him right. He had to say it a few
more times before I could take it in. He says:
"I've got you an advance of five grand"—
(which is really pretty good for a first novel)—
"and I've got the film people interested."

SPRING

I can't believe it.

TOD

But it's true! It's really true! I'm supposed to
start work with an editor at Triumph next
week. But there isn't a lot to do—just small
changes.

SPRING

Well, you've worked hard enough for it, I
must say. You deserve a lot of credit.

TOD

I can't wait to tell Grace. She'll faint, just
watch and see.

SPRING
Where did you say she went?

TOD
To Macy's. I found the note she left blown
under the table. She went up to do some
shopping. I wish she'd call so I could tell her.
She'll be the happiest gal in the world when
she hears.
	(*turns to* BUTSY)
Want another drink, er . . .

BUTSY
Fred—Fred Suddeth, but everybody calls me
Butsy on account of I smoke cigars all the
time. Boy, I really walked in on something,
didn't I?

TOD
Looks like you did, Butsy—it's going to be a
party all day—all night—all weekend, maybe!
	(TOD *goes to the kitchen area to fix*
	BUTSY *a drink. He continues to talk*
	as he does so.)
See, Mom was supposed to come over
yesterday, er—Butsy—but she never shows up
when she says she will. Hell, I got depressed
waiting for her. I was supposed to be
working—writing. But she said she'd be over,
so I didn't work.

SPRING

I just didn't have the energy.

BUTSY

I guess not. We went out dancing Thursday
night, so on Friday we—
    (*stopped by* SPRING)

TOD

(*bringing* BUTSY *his drink*)
Well, that's O.K., but why didn't you call? I
could have gone ahead with my work. I
waited all day for you. It got me all off my
schedule for nothing.

SPRING

I wasn't sure whether I'd come or not.

TOD

Well . . . Well, never mind. It's a happy day.
One of the happiest of my life.

BUTSY

What's your book about?

TOD

It's about my mother and my father and me,
growing up absurd. It's called *Neglect*.

BUTSY (*shrugging*)
I don't know nothing about books. But I can
tell you this—your Mom sure is a good
dancer.

TOD
I know. I don't think she's ever going to grow
old—or up.

SPRING
I don't want to grow up. If you grow up you
grow old and I don't have any intention of
growing old. Let's put some music on.

TOD
(*putting soft, romantic music
on record player*)
Anything to please. Can you believe it? I'm a
novelist!

SPRING
And don't forget that five thousand dollars!
But, you know, you don't seem all that excited
about it.

TOD
I'm still in shock.

BUTSY
I was in a movie once.

SPRING
(*who tends to speak over and for
others*)
Butsy's a jockey.

BUTSY
<u>Used</u> to be a jockey. Mostly nowadays I just
play the nags.

SPRING
Butsy's a sporting man.

BUTSY
Yeah, that's it. You got some Mom here, Tod.

TOD
She's a sport.

SPRING
Oooh, all this attention! I love it!

BUTSY
I met your Mom a few months ago, over in
Jersey, at a bar—a nice place, you know—and
she was behaving like a perfect lady. That's
what I said to myself—that's a perfect lady.

TOD (*kiddingly*)
Oh, she's not always such a perfect lady. Are
you, Mom?

SPRING

I hope not.

BUTSY

Hey, you shouldn't talk like that.

SPRING

Butsy's Irish.

BUTSY

She kids me about being holy. So O.K., that's
the way I was brought up. Anyhow, she's
Irish herself, ain't she? She told me that she
wanted to be a nun when she was a little girl.

TOD

She wasn't cut out for a nun.

SPRING

Let's drink to that! Let's drink to that and
then let's dance.
          (*She downs her beer and changes
          the record to dance music.*)
Come on, I want to dance with my son, the
author.
          (TOD *gets up and dances with*
          SPRING *while* BUTSY *watches,
          amused, curious, humming and puffing
          on his cigar. Mother and son are good
          dancers, but unyielding to each other's*

70

desire to lead. BUTSY *shoves his
cigar into his mouth and applauds as
the dance ends.* TOD *bows to his
mother and resumes his seat, wiping his
brow, and drinks his beer.* BUTSY *has
meantime taken to the floor to dance
with* SPRING, *who resets the record
player.* BUTSY *still holds his cigar,
puffing at it as he dances. He dances in
the style of the Forties, doing deep dips,
and whispering in* SPRING's *ear.*
TOD *watches until the dance ends, then
goes to the refrigerator and brings back
cans of beer for himself and his mother.*
BUTSY *has begun to hum "I Left My
Heart in San Francisco;" now he
drops it and begins to croon "The
Christmas Song."*

BUTSY (*singing*)
Chestnuts roasting on an open fire . . . That's
one colored guy had a beautiful voice, that Nat
Cole.

SPRING
You have a beautiful voice. Doesn't he, Tod?
Butsy's a real crooner.

TOD

I wish Grace would call. What time is it,
anyway?

BUTSY
(*looking at his watch*)
It's noon. Hey, what do you think of this
watch? It's digital. How much do you think it
cost?

TOD

I couldn't even guess.

BUTSY

Nothing. It got stuck on my wrist.

SPRING

Butsy! Listen, why don't you go and get us
some food.

BUTSY

Is there a deli around here?

TOD

Straight down the hill, two blocks. But I
should do the buying. You're my guests.
Trouble is (*laughing*) I haven't got any money.
Flat broke.

                    BUTSY
Tapped out?

                    TOD
Tap city.

                    SPRING
Butsy'll buy.

                    BUTSY
Sure. I hit it big at the track last week. I'll get
some more beer, too. Be right back.
          (*Exits*)

                    TOD
Where did you find him?

                    SPRING
Do you like him?

                    TOD
          (*laughs and shrugs*)
He's O.K.

                    SPRING
Sort of common, eh?

                    TOD
I don't think of people that way. But he's a
thief, isn't he?

SPRING

Oh, he just picks things up. He does it more
for the game. But he is a comedown from
your father, isn't he?

TOD

I'll have to admit that.

SPRING

I miss your father so. I was just thinking the
other day—it'll soon be his birthday. He died
five years ago. Where does the time go?

TOD
(*reciting spiritedly*)
Time, you old Gypsy Man,
Why hasten away?
Put up your caravan
Just for one day.

SPRING

You're so much like him.

TOD

Not much, really. He was a gentleman.

SPRING

You're a gentleman.

TOD

I can act like one when I have to. He didn't
know how not to be one, anymore than he
knew how to stay sober for thirty days in a
row.

SPRING

I loved him but I never understood him. Tod,
you don't mind me going out with other men,
do you?

TOD

Absolutely not. You have a lot of living to do.
I want you to do it.

SPRING

Then you didn't really mean what you said.

TOD

What?

SPRING

What you called me. A whore.

TOD

Of course I didn't mean it. I'm Irish too, you
know. But don't you remember what got me
started?

I know.

TOD

You didn't call me or let me know where you
were for three months. I was going crazy with
worry. I called the police. Missing persons.
The hospitals. Everyone. The Fire Depart-
ment! And all the time you were shacked up
with some guy who told you that calling me
meant that you loved me more than you did
him. It's crazy. Naturally, when you finally
did call and told me how things stood I was
upset—angry—by God, I was furious! What
did you expect? There you are, sixty-six years
old, and vanished somewhere in the wilds of
New Jersey—

SPRING

Sixty-four!

TOD

O.K., <u>sixteen</u>! My sixteen-year-old mother
vanishes one day, only to turn up three months
later, to say that her boy-friend—of whom I've
never heard—told her not to call me. A
stranger to both of us!

SPRING

I know. I was wrong. I just didn't want to cause any trouble.

TOD

Cause trouble! How do you think I felt?

SPRING

Well, let's get off that now.

TOD

Why? Just because you want to? It always has to be your way, doesn't it? To hell with me!

SPRING

Tod, let's not fight. This is a big day. You've sold your novel. Think of it! My son, the novelist!

TOD

And here I was, newly married, and I couldn't even invite my mother for a visit because I didn't know where she was. It played havoc with my nerves.

SPRING

You're not the only one with nerves.

TOD

And Grace lost the baby because of it.

SPRING

She lost the baby because of Billy Shaw. And
that happened because of your drinking.

TOD

Well, who taught me to drink? It's the only
thing I ever saw as a child. You and Dad!
Parties and dead soldiers!

SPRING

Other people survive without becoming
drunks.

TOD

Yes, if they've got something else. What did I
have? I never went to school. I had no
brothers or sisters—thanks to your abortions—
or even any friends. I was just locked up
alone with you two and your drinking. Kept
with you so you wouldn't have to worry about
me. Not even let out of those dismal apart-
ments to play on the street. At least you could
have sent me off to school in the morning.

SPRING

You know we moved too often for you to go.
We were in and out of town in a week.

TOD

There are laws.

SPRING

Oh, we got into trouble. Do you remember the
time when the truant officer came to our door
to check on you, and Dad was standing across
the street—

TOD
(*remembering, his mood lightening*)
He'd just left the house, going somewhere—

SPRING

He was going off to his territory to sell. And
when he saw this nice-looking man at our
door—

TOD (*gaily*)
He came charging back, thinking the man was
your secret lover—

SPRING

And you should have seen the look on his face
when I introduced them. "This is Mr.
Whoever-it-was, the truant officer—"

(*They break into laughter, but are
interrupted by the ringing of the
telephone.*)

TOD

That must be Grace.
     (*hurries to the phone, eager with
     his news*)
Hello. Oh, Jean. No, I thought it was Grace.
Yeah. She's gone shopping. Macy's,
Manhattan, I think. You're home early. Half
day, today? Yes, sure, come on down. We're
having a party. Yes. I have some wonderful
news. Wait till you hear. O.K., 'bye.

SPRING

What's she doing home at this hour? I thought
she did some kind of counseling or something
on Saturdays.

TOD

She does. But it was a half day today.

SPRING

Is she getting adjusted to widowhood?

TOD

I suppose so. She seems all right.

SPRING

It's easier at her age.

TOD

I don't know. Being a widow at twenty-five

TOD (*Cont'd*)
must be different from being one at sixty-five
but who can say that it's easier?

SPRING
That's right. You're very wise for such a
young man.

TOD
I'm not such a young man and I'm smart
enough, at least, to know that I'm not very
wise.

SPRING
There you go, always taking exception to
everything I say. Isn't there anything about
your old mother that you like?

TOD
(*suddenly lightening, giving her a hug*)
Why, I like everything about my not-so-old
mother.

(KNOCK at the door)

TOD
(*going to door*)
Except that she tells me one thing and does
another.

TOD (*Cont'd*)
(*holding doorknob*)
She tells me she'll be over on Friday and
makes me give up a day's work waiting—
which makes me get drunk, which gives me a
hangover—and then she shows up on Saturday
with a stranger in tow.
(*opens door*)

JEAN SHAW
Hi, Tod. Oh, hello, Mrs. Mitchell. I didn't
know you were visiting. How are you?

SPRING
Jean, you know I like you to call me Spring.
I'm fine. How're you?
(*They meet center and hug.*)

JEAN
I'm lucky today. I got off early.

SPRING
I don't know how you can stand it, being with
children all week and then again on Saturday.
I couldn't bear it. I remember—

TOD
Sit down, Jean. Want a drink? A beer?

JEAN

Yes—a beer.
>   (TOD *goes to refrigerator and brings
>   three cans of beer to table, opens them
>   and pours a round while* SPRING
>   *speaks.*)

SPRING

Well, I had six little sisters and brothers and
one older sister who refused to do a thing. We
were very poor. Our father had died at only
twenty-nine—and Mama worked as a cook in
a girls' school and was away most of the time
and it fell to me to take care of all those kids—
and I used to say to myself: Spring, I'd say,
when you grow up don't you ever be such a
fool as to get married and have children. I
even thought I might become a nun.

TOD

But you didn't. You got married and had me.

SPRING

Well, yes. I fell in love with your father.
That's what kind of fool I am, as the song
says.

TOD

Thanks a lot.

SPRING

Well, I didn't mean—

TOD

Of course not. How do you think it makes me
feel every time you say that? I've heard it all
my life.

SPRING

You know I don't mean . . . That's just the
way I chatter on. I don't mean anything.

TOD

You don't think about the way you make other
people feel.

SPRING

Oh, let's get off me. Tell Jean the news.

JEAN

Yes, what is it?

SPRING

Tod sold his book.

JEAN

Oh, Tod! How wonderful! Have you told
Grace? What did she do?

TOD

She doesn't know yet.

SPRING

She's been out all day.

JEAN

Oh, I've got to stay and see her reaction. I
know she'll be in her glory.

SPRING

Yes, Grace has been a good wife.

JEAN

She always believed in you. So did I. And so
did Billy.

SPRING

So did I.

TOD

You!

SPRING

Well I did. Of course I did.

TOD

I don't know how you could have. After
depriving me of any education whatsoever,

TOD (*Cont'd*)

you told me I couldn't be a writer because I
didn't have any education.

SPRING

Well, I didn't know anything about those
things. I had to leave school in the sixth grade
to go to work in a mill. You should have
asked your father. He was the big brain. He
went to college.

TOD

Dreiser's mother didn't know anything about
those things either. He had to teach her to
read. But she said that he could be or do
anything he wanted to be or do. She didn't
constantly put him down all through his
childhood in order to exalt her own feeble ego.
Vanity! All is vanity!

SPRING
(*to* JEAN)

Let's ignore him. He's drunk.

JEAN

Let's do. Until he cheers up.

(KNOCK *at the door*)

SPRING

That must be Butsy.

(*She goes to door, opens it, admitting*
BUTSY, *who is carrying an enormous
load of groceries in his arms. Behind
him* DELIVERY BOY *enters pushing a
shopping cart filled to brimming.*)

What's this? Where have you been so long?

BUTSY

I've been shopping. Come on in, kid. Push it
in here.

SPRING

What did you get?

BUTSY

I got some of everything. I mean, this is a
party, ain't it?

(TOD *and* JEAN *help* BUTSY *with his
bags.* BUTSY *and* SPRING *and the*
DELIVERY BOY *unload the
shopping cart.*)

SPRING

Stuffed artichoke hearts! Canned lobster!
Crabmeat!

BUTSY

How did they get in there? I don't remember

                    BUTSY (*Cont'd*)
payin' for them.

                    SPRING
Butsy, you didn't!

                    BUTSY
Here kid, buy yourself a chocolate cigar.

                    DELIVERY BOY
Gee, thanks, Mister.

                    BUTSY
More where that came from, kid.
          (DELIVERY BOY *Exits*)
Sure I did. I got plenty to spend—easy come,
easy go—and I don't mind spendin' it; but
those supermarkets are a bunch of crooks.
You think I should pay for lobster at their
prices when the lobsters are running all over
the ocean? Look!
          (*taking more canned goods from his
          pockets and from under and inside
          his jacket*)
Butsy's got the magic touch.

                    SPRING
Butsy's got light fingers. What do you think
Tod and Jean must think of you?

TOD (*perversely*)

I'm with Butsy. The supermarkets are a bunch
of crooks. They take us, we should take them.
More power to you, Butsy!

JEAN

Me too.

BUTSY

There, you see? They think I did right.

SPRING

But suppose you got caught?

BUTSY

Hell, I been lifting stuff all my life and never
got caught yet.

SPRING

There's always a first time.

BUTSY

They only warn you the first time. Gimme a
drink, will you, somebody? That hill's a hot
climb.

TOD

Butsy, this is a friend of ours—Jean Shaw.
Jean lives upstairs. Jean, Fred Suddeth, a
friend of Mom's.

BUTSY

Nice meetin' ya.

JEAN

Same here—er . . . .

SPRING
(*putting groceries away*)
Call him Butsy.

BUTSY

Yeah—call me Butsy. Everybody does.

JEAN

That's an unusual name.

BUTSY

Because—see—
(*lighting a cigar*)

JEAN

Ah! What do you do, Butsy?

SPRING

Butsy's a jockey.

BUTSY

<u>Was</u> a jockey. Now I'm a sporting man.
Anybody can see I'm too old to be a jockey—
and too fat. She's always building me up to

BUTSY (*Cont'd*)

her friends. What do you think? Something
wrong with what I am?

JEAN

Not that I can see.

BUTSY

Hey, I like this one. You I like. Good-lookin'
too.

SPRING (*kiddingly*)

Watch out there.

JEAN

You better watch out, Spring. Butsy is very
handsome—in a rugged, red-headed way. My
husband, Billy, was a red-head.

BUTSY

That right? Oh, I'm old enough to be your
father.

SPRING

(*still busy with the groceries*)
Grandfather, you mean.

BUTSY

I wouldn't say that. She's always tearing me
down.

JEAN
I thought she was always building you up.

BUTSY
Well, like this, see: building up what I do,
tearing down what I am.

TOD
(*has returned to his seat and is
drinking beer and smoking a
cigarette, looking gloomy*)
I know the feeling.

JEAN
What <u>do</u> you do, Butsy? What's a sporting
man?

TOD
Butsy's a gambler, I think.

BUTSY
Spring, you got a sharp son here.

TOD
Nothing sharp about it. You said you were
flush from the track.

BUTSY
Did I? I get a few drinks, I forget.

SPRING

Butsy, did you stop off along the way?
          (*putting the last of the
          groceries away*)
I think you stopped off and had a few somewhere. Shopping should have cleared your
head.

BUTSY

Well, I hadda, Christsake! Oops! Shouldn't
take the name of the Lord in vain. I mean,
here I am all of a sudden sitting around with a
guy who writes books—me, who on'y reads
the headlines and funnies and sports pages of
the Daily News. I'm nervous.

SPRING

You? Nervous?

BUTSY

Yeah—me—nervous! I'm human, you know.
          (*To* TOD)
All the way over here from Jersey I'm
thinking: I got to behave very elegant now
because I'm meetin' Spring's son who is a
writer. And I got nervous.

TOD

Are you nervous now?

BUTSY

Now? Not so much now. First thing I see you
drinking beer I say to myself: This is a regular
guy.

SPRING

I told you Tod wasn't a snob.

TOD

But <u>you</u> are.

BUTSY

Aw, no. Don't talk unpleasant to your Mom.
Look, Tod: I know I ain't got no education;
but that don't mean I haven't learned something. And one thing I know is: a mother is
the most wonderful thing in the world.

SPRING

Bravo!
          (*She joins them at the table.*)
I told you he was an Irishman.

BUTSY

Hey, look at the Irish mug on her! I'm nuts
about your Mom, Tod. She's what I call a
lady.

SPRING

Well, thank you.

BUTSY

And you too—what'd you say your name
was?

JEAN

Jean.

BUTSY

That's a pretty name. Hey, it seems to me like
you said your husband was dead. Did I get
that right?

JEAN

Yes, he's dead.

TOD

I was with him. It was an accident.

BUTSY (*interested*)

Yeah? What kind of an accident? Oh, listen, I
don't mean to make you talk about it if—

JEAN

No, it's all right . . . I've got to get used to it.

TOD

We were out drinking together. Billy was my
best friend. We'd been drinking all day . . . I
tried to get him to come home but he didn't
want to quit. Finally, I got him into the

TOD (*Cont'd*)

subway, but he darted for a car and the doors
closed before I could get on. The next
morning he was found dead at a distant stop.
He'd apparently fallen down a flight of iron
stairs.

SPRING

Tod—

TOD (*to* JEAN)

Are you—

JEAN

No, I'm all right. That's what happened. He
had red hair, too, like yours, Butsy.

TOD

He was a musician.

SPRING

A classical musician.

BUTSY

Classical. Gee, I'm sorry.

JEAN

Come on, let's cheer up.

SPRING

I've got an idea.

JEAN

What?

SPRING

Let's surprise Grace. You and I and the boys
can get the place all spruced up—

TOD (*cheering*)

A real party! And thanks to Butsy we've got
everything we need.

JEAN (*enthusiastically*)

We should decorate the place.

BUTSY

Yeah, like Christmas!

JEAN

That's it. We'll get out the Christmas decorations—chains and lights and everything and
really make it look like a party.

SPRING

Then when Grace walks in we'll all shout:
Tod's novel is going to be published!

JEAN

Billy would have loved this so much. He
thought you were a fine writer, Tod.

TOD

He would have become a great musician.

JEAN

Oh, what a wonderful idea, Spring! Come on,
let's get started.

SPRING

I'll do the dirty dishes and clean up and you
start hanging the decorations. Don't forget the
lights! I love bright, pretty lights!

TOD

What should I do?

JEAN

Nothing. What do you think this party's
about? You're the one who wrote the book.
You and Grace.

TOD

I'd never have done it if it hadn't been for her.

SPRING

She always believed in you.

BUTSY

She must be a great gal. Hey, what should I
do?

SPRING

You keep Tod company. Show him some of
your card tricks.

TOD (*dreamily*)

She's the only person who ever helped or
encouraged me.

SPRING

Let's get busy.
>(*JEAN goes upstairs for Christmas
decorations. SPRING goes to kitchen
area and begins to do dishes. BUTSY
takes a package of playing cards from
an inside pocket, breaks the seal, and
begins methodically shuffling the
cards, the while puffing on his teeth-
clenched cigar and watching SPRING
admiringly.*)

TOD

(*stares into space, sips his beer
and mutters*)
I've done it! I'm a novelist!

BUTSY
(*ignoring* TOD, *watching* SPRING
as she works)
Ain't she something? Ain't she something?

(JEAN *enters carrying a large box of
Christmas decorations and sets to
work. She has left the door open and a
stooped, gaunt, once-beautiful old
woman enters, leaning on a cane.*)

SOPHIA BENNETT
(*in a cultured, British accent*)
What's this? It isn't Christmas yet, is it? I
feel like Rip Van Winkle.

TOD
(*rising and going to meet* SOPHIA)
Sophia, I've had wonderful news! My novel's
been accepted by Triumph.

SOPHIA

Really?

JEAN
We're going to have a party. Oh, you know
Tod's mother, Sophia. And this is Mister—

BUTSY (*rising*)
Butsy. Do you live here, too?

SOPHIA

(*nodding to* SPRING)

How do you do, Mister Butsy? Yes,
downstairs.

SPRING

Mister Suddeth. His nickname is Butsy.

SOPHIA

(*being seated with* TOD's *help*)

Suddeth? What an odd name! Is it English?

BUTSY

Irish-American. Are you English?

SOPHIA

Welsh—so you see you needn't be defensive.
Jean is Irish too. We are all Celts here. Congratulations, Tod! How wonderful for you! I
can imagine how happy Gracie must be.

TOD

She doesn't know yet. She went off to Macy's
before I got the news.

JEAN

It'll be a surprise party for her.

SPRING

Would you like a drink, Sophia?

SOPHIA

Yes, a whiskey and soda—no ice—thank you,
Spring. You must be very proud of Tod. This
is his red letter day.

SPRING
(getting drink)
I certainly am.

BUTSY

She was telling me all about him on the way
over from Jersey . . . I was sort of scared to
meet a writer until she told me what a regular
guy he was—how he was a shoeshine boy as a
kid—like me—and had been in the Marines
and all. She said how he never had no
education to speak of, how he educated
himself. We're from the school of hard
knocks, ain't we, Tod?

SOPHIA

Tod is a very well-educated man.

JEAN
(tacking up Christmas tree lights)
Sophia is a writer, too, Butsy—a poet—

TOD

And an actress. She once worked with Leslie
Howard on the stage. Do you know him?

BUTSY

The English actor who was with Bogart in
"Petrified Forest." Sure, I know all Bogey's
movies. I started to say before how I was in a
movie. It was "High Sierra," where I did the
fall for Bogart. You know. When he rolls
down the mountain. That was me rolling.

SOPHIA

You were a stuntman?

SPRING

He's more of a story-teller. He's making that
up.

BUTSY

I did some stunt work. I told you. Before I
was a jockey.

SOPHIA

That's very interesting. What do you do now?

SPRING

He's a sporting man.
          (*gives* SOPHIA *her drink and sits
          down with the others*)

BUTSY

I'm a gambler.

JEAN

I like to gamble.

SPRING

So do I. It's fun.

SOPHIA (*kiddingly*)

Ah, Monte Carlo when I was a young thing!

TOD

Not me. I want something I can count on.

SOPHIA

But you've gambled all along. You've gambled on yourself, and your very life! And you've won!

BUTSY

Yeah, that's a way of looking at it!

SOPHIA

Three cheers for Tod!

ALL TOGETHER

Hip, hip, hurray!   Hip, hip, hurray! Hip, hip, hurray!

(*they applaud*)

(END OF ACT)

ACT II

SETTING: Evening and the apartment is illuminated by lamps and Christmas lights, which reflect on the highly-colored ornaments and baubles that hang about from chains of popcorn and paper, lending the drunken scene a harsh, garish appearance. JEAN is dancing with BUTSY, and SPRING is dancing with TOD. SOPHIA looks on, tapping the floor with her cane.

AT RISE: A record is coming to its end, and the dancers sit down to their drinks.

SPRING

Enough!

TOD

Too much!

SPRING

   (*to* JEAN)
Isn't Butsy a wonderful dancer!

105

JEAN

He's a dream!

SOPHIA

I wonder where Grace is. It's dark outside.

JEAN

We've been at it for hours. Isn't anybody
getting hungry?

SPRING

Let's bring out the food. Grace can eat when
she gets here. She won't mind if we don't
wait for her.

TOD

I'd like to wait for her. She won't be much
longer.

SPRING

She won't mind. Help me, Jean. We'll make
a nice crabmeat salad.

(SPRING *and* JEAN *go to kitchen
area and start work.*)

BUTSY

Your Mom just can't wait for anybody. I'm
always running after her. When I say, "Why
can't you wait for me?"—you know what she

106

BUTSY (*Cont'd*)

says? "I'm an individual." I don't even know
what she means. She's really something!
Ain't she something, Tod?

SOPHIA

Why?

BUTSY

Why what?

SOPHIA

Why do you run after her?

BUTSY

Because I'm crazy about her. What do you
think? She's a free spirit. Don't like to be
pinned down.

SOPHIA

That's a bit irresponsible, isn't it?

BUTSY

Hey, wait a minute. She don't have to answer
to nobody.

SOPHIA

She doesn't <u>have</u> to, but shouldn't she? I
know of several times when Tod has stopped

SOPHIA (*Cont'd*)
working because he expected a visit from his
mother and then she didn't show up.

BUTSY
That's her business, ain't it?

SOPHIA
No. If you make an appointment and someone
stops what he's doing because of it and then
you don't meet him or call him up and explain,
I'd say it had become his business. Tod is a
writer. His work requires concentration and
good work habits. It requires self-discipline,
and that sort of thing is very distracting and
weakening. Too much interruption can
damage a work, or even damage the writer. I
know. I write myself. And I wouldn't allow
anyone to do that to me. Tod's patience
amazes me.

BUTSY
(*to* TOD)
Is this lady a good friend of yours?

SPRING
(*coming to table*)
If I ever do that, it's between my son and me,
and I'll thank you to mind your own business.

SOPHIA (*undaunted*)

Tod is a good son. I know how unhappy you
sometimes make him. I've seen him put his
very important work aside and sit in expecta-
tion of one of your visits. Then you not show
up. You don't seem to understand what it
does to him.

SPRING

Who are you? You have no business here
anyway, you old drunkard.

BUTSY

Don't get sore at the old douche-bag, Spring.
What a temper! Ain't she something?

SPRING

No! She can't talk to me like that in my son's
house.

TOD

Nevertheless, she's telling the truth. Suppose
I had been working today. You had no way of
knowing I wasn't, but you barge in anyhow,
without any warning, and even bring
company. I waited for you all day yesterday.
And nobody showed up or even called.

SPRING

I've explained that.

BUTSY

Your Mom explained that. Remember, your mother is the best friend you'll ever have. I know my mother is.

TOD

I don't know about your mother, but mine has been driving me crazy ever since I can remember. That's what my novel is all about—my playboy father and my merry mother. They were both so damned gay! Except when my father was staggering around for weeks on end in his shitty undershorts and my mother was screaming at him until I thought my eardrums would break. They were irresponsible, that's what they were! Selfish and irresponsible!

JEAN
(*who has been listening and now
comes to join the group at the table*)
I'm not so sure you have any right to talk about anybody being irresponsible, Tod. If you had been more responsible, maybe Billy would still be here.

(*She begins to cry.* TOD *sits, shaken
and staring.* SPRING, BUTSY *and*
SOPHIA *gather around* JEAN,
comforting her.)

SOPHIA

She's had a little too much to drink, I think.

BUTSY

Naw. She <u>needs</u> a drink.

SPRING
(*to* JEAN)
Come and sit down at the table.

SOPHIA

Mister Butsy, I wonder if you would be so
kind as to go to the liquor store for me. If you
would get me a pint of whiskey—I'd like to go
to my own apartment.
(*She waves out a bill.*)

SPRING
(*still comforting* JEAN)
Get it for her, Butsy.
(BUTSY *takes money and exits.*)

JEAN
(*suddenly out of control*)
He killed my husband! He took him out and
killed him!

TOD

You know damn well that isn't true, Jean!

JEAN

It is true! Billy had a brilliant career ahead of
him, and now he's dead!

TOD

You know as well as I do that Billy was an
alcoholic. He was reckless. He was picked up
by the police where he had fallen many a time.
He was always bruised and banged up from
falling down.

JEAN

But you had him stay with you and drink that
day and then you let him get away and die—

TOD

I was too drunk—

JEAN

Well, isn't that irresponsible?

TOD

Well, aren't you drunk now? Didn't you ever
drink with him? It just <u>happened</u> to happen
when he was with me.

JEAN

Is that how you explain it to yourself?

TOD (*hesitating*)

No.

SPRING

She's just upset, Tod. She doesn't mean what she's saying.

SOPHIA

To hear you, nobody means what he or she is saying. I can assure you that I generally do. But she doesn't <u>know</u> what she's saying.

TOD

(*bucking up*)

Billy's death wasn't any more my fault because he had gone out with me than it would have been your fault if he had gone out with you.

JEAN

He never died with me. Somebody's got to be responsible for something!

SPRING

Here, have another drink. Now drink it slowly.

SOPHIA

She should have some coffee. Tod, why don't you recite a poem? Tod's a wonderful reader.

113

SPRING

Oh, I don't want to hear any of that. This is
supposed to be a party.

JEAN
(*drying her eyes*)
No, let him. I like to listen to him recite.

TOD

I don't feel like it.

JEAN

Please, Tod. I'm sorry for what I said. I don't
know what comes over me. Billy loved to
hear you read poetry.

SPRING

It's boring. It's very boring when you are
trying to have fun.

SOPHIA

Well, it <u>is</u> his party. Recite something for us,
Tod.

TOD

Yeah—O.K. I've got just the number for this
occasion.
(*He goes to bookcase and withdraws
book, stands to recite.*)
This is by Poe. It's called "To My Mother—"

SPRING
Is this going to be insulting? Because if it is—

TOD
I don't see how anybody can be insulted by
this. Why be defensive? Do you feel guilty?
          (*he recites*—)

Because I feel that, in the heavens above,
The angels, whispering to one another,
Can find, among their burning terms of love,
None so devotional as that of "Mother,"
Therefore by that dear name I long have called
          you—
You who are more than mother unto me,
And fill my heart of hearts, where Death
          installed you,
In setting my Virginia's spirit free.
My mother—my own mother, who died early,
Was but the mother of myself; but you
Are mother to the one I loved so dearly,
And thus are dearer than the mother I knew
By that infinity with which my wife
Was dearer to my soul than its soul life.

          (BUTSY *has entered during the*
          reading and is waiting at the door,
          bottle in bag in hand, listening, and
          puffing on his cigar. Now he steps
          forward.)

115

BUTSY

Now that's the right way to talk to your
mother.

SOPHIA
(*rising to meet* BUTSY)
Thank you for that good reading, Tod. It was
beautiful!
(*takes bag from* BUTSY *and
goes to door, tapping her cane*)

BUTSY

Your change.

SOPHIA

Please keep it for your trouble. Good evening.
And congratulations again, Tod! I knew that
wonderful novel would be snatched up by
somebody.
(*Exits*)

BUTSY

Keep it for my trouble! She gave me a tip,
like I was an errand boy! The nerve of the old
douche-bag!

SPRING

Sit down, Butsy! That poem was beautiful,
Tod. Thank you.

TOD

What for? I don't think you understood it, did
you?

SPRING

Now don't start on me again, just when I
thought you'd stopped.

BUTSY

You know, that poem makes me think of how
I haven't called my Mom in a long time. I
think it's been a year. She's nearly ninety.
She won't be around much longer.

SPRING

Now don't go getting sentimental. Let's have
some fun, for God's sake! Put the dance
music back on, Tod! I just love to dance,
don't you, Jean?

JEAN

I loved to dance with Billy. He was a wonderful dancer.

BUTSY

How 'bout me?

SPRING

Butsy is a wonderful dancer.

JEAN (*dreamily*)
And red-headed, like Billy.

BUTSY
Is she flirting with me? Are you flirting with
me, girly?

SPRING
The vanity of men! You old fool, she's young
enough to be your granddaughter!

BUTSY
My daughter, maybe. Don't forget, I'm a lot
younger than you are.

SPRING
Oh, thanks a lot. But you aren't <u>that</u> much
younger.

BUTSY
I can't stop thinking about my mother. It
comes to me sometimes that maybe she's dead
already, and I don't know it.

SPRING
Doesn't your brother live with her? He'd tell
you if anything had happened to her.

BUTSY
Maybe not. I'm the bum in the family. They

BUTSY (*Cont'd*)
don't care what I know. The last time I saw
my brother, I tried to put the touch on him for
a few hundred—he's a contractor and he's got
the money—and he wouldn't give me a dime.
He tried to throw me out, but I bopped him
one on the nose. I broke his beak for him,
that's what I did. No; maybe he wouldn't tell
me.

JEAN
I thought you were a jockey, not a boxer.

BUTSY
I fought feather weight in the Golden Gloves
before I was a jockey.

JEAN
Was that before you were a stuntman?

BUTSY
Yeah. But suppose Momma's dead?

TOD
If you want to, you can call her up from here.
The phone's over there.

BUTSY
Gee—thanks, Tod—but no. I'm afraid she
might be dead. I don't want to know.

JEAN

That's the way I felt when Billy was missing.

TOD

I was home, drunk, asleep. I didn't know until
the next day. He was still alive, in intensive
care, when I went to see him. Unconscious.
He died a few hours later. I didn't want to
know, either, when he died.

SPRING

When my husband was missing—in the fire—
I was glad when he wasn't immediately
identified. There was a chance, then. But I
knew he was dead. Tod finally identified him
at the morgue.

TOD
(*to* BUTSY)
He was living in an old fire trap rooming
house in Newark. It was filled with derelicts
and drunks like himself. Six of them died.

SPRING

We had had an argument and he had moved
down there—but he would have come back as
soon as he sobered up.

TOD

He told me that he was never going back to

TOD (*Cont'd*)
you. He said he wanted some peace.
          (*to* BUTSY)
He was an old man, much older than Mom is
now, and that was five years ago. I was a late
child. He had had another son, by a former
marriage, and I don't think he ever really
wanted me, though he loved me well enough
in his way, I guess. I don't think he wanted to
have any children by Mom. I was an accident.

SPRING
You were not. He let me have you because I
wanted you. He had had me aborted twice
before.

BUTSY
Jesus, Mary and Joseph, don't say it!

SPRING
He didn't mean it about not coming back.

TOD
He said you drove him crazy.

SPRING
Well, he drove <u>me</u> crazy.

TOD
But he was drunk. You were sober by then. If

TOD (*Cont'd*)
you had only let him be, he wouldn't have
gone to that firetrap to find some peace.

BUTSY
What if she's dead?
(BUTSY *begins to cry. JEAN rises
suddenly, crying hysterically, and
runs out of the apartment.*)

SPRING
(*as* TOD *starts to go after* JEAN)
Let her go. She'll feel better if she gets it out
of her system.

BUTSY
But what if Mamma is dead?

SPRING
She isn't dead!

TOD
Call her up.

BUTSY
It's long distance—California. But I'll pay for
the call. Could I?

TOD
Go ahead.

(BUTSY *goes to thephone and, taking it, sits on the couch, drawing out an address book. He starts to place the call.*)

SPRING

Your father would have come back to me, and it was cruel of you to say that he wouldn't.

TOD

Cruel! Don't you think the things you do— and always have done—are cruel? All you ever say is how I took fifteen hours to be born, and how agonizing it was for you.

SPRING

Well, that's the truth!

TOD

But do you have to tell me it every time we have a drink together?

SPRING

Well, what's it got to do with you? I was the one who was in pain.

TOD

I didn't want to come out and meet you!

SPRING

That's a rotten thing to say to your mother!

BUTSY

(*into telephone*)
Momma? Momma?

SPRING

You're just drunk! You've turned out to be a
drunk like your father.

TOD

How else could I turn out? It's all I've ever
known.

BUTSY

She's dead! She's dead, Spring! What?

SPRING

You should respect your mother!

TOD

There's nothing to respect!

BUTSY

Please, somebody—my Mamma's dead!
What? What?

SPRING

Oh, for God's sake! Help him, Tod. Stop

SPRING (*Cont'd*)
<u>crying</u> Butsy! Tod, take that phone away from
him!

TOD
(*taking phone from* BUTSY)
I'm a friend of—what? Oh, I see. Yes. Yes,
he's had a few. Butsy, your mother is in bed.
She's fine. She's taking a nap. Here—
(*hands* BUTSY *the phone*)

BUTSY
Hello?

SPRING
(*seating herself at table*)
I don't know why you hate me so much. I've
always been a good mother.

TOD
Which is why I was dragged all over the
country and never got any schooling. You
should have seen to it that I was taken care of.
It was your responsibility. People have no
right to have a kid and then to just pretend he
isn't there.

SPRING
That was your father's fault. I had to go
where he went. I didn't have any money.

SPRING (*Cont'd*)

Other women have had it easier.

TOD

Other women have worked. You could have
worked. You could have made a real home for
us, even if it was just a little apartment.

SPRING

What's the use of re-hashing all this now?
That's all in the past.

TOD

No, it isn't. It's in the present. I'm still
paying for it.

SPRING

Have you forgotten what this party is about?
Your novel is going to be published. You're
successful, so what difference does it make or
not make what I did or didn't do?

TOD

It makes a difference that I've been a nervous
wreck all my life. That I haven't been suited
for a normal life. That I've never been able to
get a decent job. That, if this novel hadn't
been accepted, eventually I would have killed
myself.

SPRING

Don't say that! You're just being dramatic!

TOD

You damned old selfish insensitive bitch! All
you've ever cared about was some paltry
comfort and a good time to break the
monotony!

BUTSY

(*turning back to* TOD *and* SPRING)
Mamma's alive! I talked to her!

GRACE MITCHELL

(*coming in door, carrying bundles*)
Well, what's happening here? What's this, a
party? Hello, Mom!
(*to* BUTSY)
Hello, there!
(*She places her bundles on couch.*)

SPRING

Grace, this is my friend, Fred Suddeth. Fred,
my daughter-in-law, Grace.

BUTSY

Call me Butsy.
(*He holds out his cigar with one hand
and points to it with the other.*)

GRACE

Hello, Butsy!

TOD

(*goes to* GRACE, *puts his arms
around her*)
Grace, I've got great news!

SPRING

Tod's novel has been accepted. Isn't it
wonderful?

(GRACE *looks at* TOD, *goes to table,
sits down. The others wait for her
reaction. She turns to* TOD, *smiling
through tears.*)

GRACE

Whoopee! Honey, you did it! I can't believe
it! Tell me all about it!

SPRING

Jerry called him this morning. He's got Tod a
five thousand dollar advance.

GRACE

Money! We've even got money! Oh, Tod,
I'm so proud!
(*She goes to him and they kiss.*)

SPRING
Would you like a drink, Grace?

GRACE
You know, Mom, I think I will have one for
once, maybe two, maybe more—to celebrate.
          (*To* BUTSY)
Tod's always complaining that I don't drink
with him. Well, this is an occasion! Did you
tell Sophia and Jean?

TOD
They were here. Jean did the decorating. Like
it?

GRACE
          (*looking around*)
She must have been drunk.

SPRING
          (*bringing drink*)
And I did the cleaning.

GRACE
Oh, thanks so much, Mom. Well, cheers!

SPRING

Cheers!

BUTSY

Cheers!

TOD

To you, honey! For believing in me like
nobody else ever has!

SPRING

Oh, that's meant for me.

BUTSY

You shouldn't be mean to your Mom, Tod.
Look how good I feel because my mother is
alive. She's nearly ninety!

TOD

She was probably a good mother.

BUTSY

(*sitting down, joined by others*)
She done her best. My old man was a beast.
He threw me out when I was fourteen.

TOD

I thought it was your brother.

BUTSY

That was later. I already had practice by that
time. That's what I said to my brother before I

BUTSY (*Cont'd*)

broke his beak; I said I should be doin' this to
the old man.
>   (*laughs*)
I just now asked my brother on the phone how
his nose feels, does it still hurt—I hope. But
what could my mother do?

TOD

She could have stopped him from throwing
you out at fourteen.

BUTSY

Naw, them were different times.

TOD

All times should be the same when it comes to
that.

GRACE

What's this all about?

SPRING

He's picking on me again.

BUTSY

You shouldn't pick on Spring. Just look at
her! Ain't she cute? Ain't she something? I
love that woman! She's a real individual! I

BUTSY (*Cont'd*)
love your mother, Tod. I don't think you
should pick on her.

TOD
It's between us.

BUTSY
No, it isn't. Not when I'm here.

GRACE
Now wait, both of you! This is a party!

TOD
Why don't you both go!

SPRING
All right. I'll be glad to go.

TOD
You aren't even supposed to be here. You
were supposed to be here yesterday.

BUTSY
I can't let you act like this, Tod. I want you to
apologize to Spring.

TOD
Go to hell!

(To cries of "Stop!" from the women,
TOD *and* BUTSY *get into a drunken
shoving match.* TOD *loses his balance
and falls, cracking his head on the
floor.)*

GRACE
(drops, kneeling, lifting TOD's *head)*
Tod! Tod! Wake up!

SPRING
Your dress is all blood! He's bleeding!

BUTSY
Christ, I'm sorry! Heads bleed something
awful. He's O.K..

GRACE
It's his ears. There's blood coming out of his
ears! Oh, God! Tod? Tod? Wake up, honey!

BUTSY
Lemme see.
        (BUTSY *feels* TOD's *heart.)*
I don't feel it. Christ, he's dead, I think!
Christ, Spring, I didn't do nothing but push
him. I didn't mean it. You know I didn't
mean it. Jesus, Mary and Joseph! Oh, Christ!
I'll see you later, Spring.
        (Exits)

SPRING
(hysterically, while GRACE *rocks*
TOD *in her arms)*
Call the hospital! Do something! Somebody,
do something!

(Sudden, complete blackout)

(CURTAIN)

A MAN OF CONSCIENCE

<u>Cast of Characters</u>

Terrorist: A man, about thirty.

Punisher: A man, about forty.

<u>Scene</u>

A windowless room, anywhere, empty but for
a straight-backed wooden chair, in which
TERRORIST is tied, and a desk, upon which
PUNISHER sits. PUNISHER hefts a long-
barrelled, powerful revolver. On the desk are
a pitcher of water and a machine-pistol.

<u>Time</u>

The present.

SETTING: A windowless room, any-
                   where, empty but for a
                   straight-backed wooden
                   chair, in which
                   TERRORIST is tied, and
                   a desk, upon which
                   PUNISHER sits.
                   PUNISHER hefts a long-
                   barreled, powerful
                   revolver. On the desk are
                   a pitcher of water and a
                   machine-pistol.

AT RISE: TERRORIST is waking.

PUNISHER

Awake?

TERRORIST
(*looking around*)
Where am I? Who are you?
(*realizes he's tied up*)
What's this? (*outraged*) Who are you? What
is this?

PUNISHER

I'm your punisher.

TERRORIST
My what? Who in hell are you?

PUNISHER
I told you, I'm your punisher.

TERRORIST
        (*to himself*)
My punisher. . .
        (*to* PUNISHER)
For what? And who in hell are you to punish
me? (*thinks*) Some damn fascist cop? Where
is this place? How did I get here?

PUNISHER
This is Purgatory. You're on your way to hell.

TERRORIST (*tough*)
What then, are you some damn loony repre-
sentative of the Church? An agent for the
Vatican or something? I don't have to tell
you, do I, that I don't believe in hell?
        (*laughs*)
Thank God!
        (*laughs again*)

PUNISHER (*slowly*)
Oh. Oh. I assure you, you're going to hell.

TERRORIST
You know it then?

PUNISHER
It? What?

TERRORIST
Hell.

PUNISHER
I can guess.

TERRORIST
Now look, you. Enough of these crazy
metaphysics. Who are you and—

PUNISHER
I'm not being metaphysical.

TERRORIST
(*not comprehending*)
What are you talking about?

PUNISHER
I mean that I've been thinking about it for a
long time. And I guess there's a hell. Maybe
not in the earth, but on the surface of it. And
that's where you're going.

TERRORIST
(*thinks maybe he's dealing with
a maniac*)
Now look, just explain to me why do you have
me tied up in this room? Tell me who you are.

PUNISHER (*dreamlike*)
Who you are. Who I am.

TERRORIST (*angry*)
Damned maniac!

PUNISHER (*calmly*)
Yes. I used to think you were the maniac.
Maybe you are. But it won't change anything.
I'm . . .
(*searches for a word, finds it, smiles*)
implacable. But I know who you are. You, in
particular. But I know who you all are.

TERRORIST (*thinking*)
All right. I think I've got it now.
(*wriggles around in his bonds*)
Oh, damn, I've got a headache! What did you
give me? Damn my head aches! Now. You
must be . . .oh. . .some kind of agent. . .CIA. . .
military. This is an interrogation. . . you want
information. . . is that it?

PUNISHER

No.

TERRORIST

No? Look, maybe I can help you. Give you
some information. What is it you want?

PUNISHER

At first I thought I wanted you dead. But as I
thought about it I realized that would be no
punishment for you. It would only set you
free.

TERRORIST

(*looking up, apprehensive*)
Revenge?

PUNISHER

I suppose so. But the more I thought about
that the less important it seemed. Anyway,
revenge should be taken in hot blood. There's
satisfaction in that. There's no satisfaction in
what I'm going to do. Indeed, I've con-
demned myself to a life of misery.

TERRORIST

Not revenge? Not revenge? Not revenge?
(*almost to himself*)
What then? What are you going on about?
(*thinks*)

TERRORIST (*Cont'd*)
What do you mean, condemn yourself to a life
of misery?
(*thinks again*)
Why?

PUNISHER
I'm a man of conscience.

TERRORIST (*spits*)
Conscience!
(*thinks for a few moments*)
Look, are you some kind of madman, or what?
Is there any water here? Can I have an
aspirin? I feel nauseous. What did you give
me, anyway? It's all a blank. I don't even
remember where I was. How long was I out?

PUNISHER
Aah. I wonder.

TERRORIST
Now what's that supposed to mean?

PUNISHER
I've been thinking about you for a long time.
Suppose we say . . . suppose we say that I'm
the husband of the secretary whose hands were
blown off, opening one of your letter bombs.

142

TERRORIST

Are you?

PUNISHER

(*Gets up. Puts revolver on desk, next to automatic. Fishes in desk drawer. Brings out bottle of whiskey, aspirin, a couple of glasses. Pours whiskey. Takes aspirin from tin. Appears thoughtful. Crosses to stand in front of* TERRORIST)

No. Open your mouth.

(*Puts two aspirin on* TERRORIST's *tongue. Holds glass of water to let* TERRORIST *drink. Withdraws glass.*)

And yes.

TERRORIST

(*choking on aspirin*)

Now what's that supposed to mean?

PUNISHER

(*going back to desk, facing* TERRORIST)

It means that it might be the case, but it's no longer the major reason. It means, as I said before, vengeance should be taken in hot blood. It means that right after your plastique blew my old father to pieces in Dublin I wanted to kill you. In hot blood! I wanted

143

PUNISHER (*Cont'd*)

revenge. Vengeance! Who wouldn't. But I
cooled off. It means that after my friend Izak,
the great Olympic runner, had his legs severed
by a blast of machine gun fire in an airport. . . .
It means that I wanted revenge for Izak! It
means that I wanted to kill you. In hot blood!
But I cooled off. It means that after my thirty
daughters ranging in age from nine to ninety
were blown up in a hotel room in Paris—I
wanted to kill you! In hot blood! But I cooled
off. I cooled off.

TERRORIST

I don't know what you're talking about.
You're completely mad.

PUNISHER

Am I?
    (*looks at* TERRORIST)
Have I become mad? Might be.
    (*shakes his head, thinking about it*)
Ask any psychiatrist. Madness is contagious.
If I'm mad it's because you're mad. If I'm
sane, you're sane, too. If we're both sane,
then there must be evil. If there is evil, there
must be good. I've thought of all this.
Finally, I don't know what to make of it. I'm
not a philosopher. I'm a . . .

TERRORIST
(*looks up, interested, fascinated.
Waits*)
Go on, a what?

PUNISHER (*shrugs*)
Can't make any difference, really. I've been a
soldier.

TERRORIST
Aaah. Now we're getting somewhere.

PUNISHER
Oh, well, we're not really getting to anything
in the sense that you mean. Who hasn't been a
soldier? In a world where you exist, everyone's a soldier in your world.

TERRORIST
What do you mean, my world?

PUNISHER
I said before, I'm a man of conscience.

TERRORIST
(*struggling in his bonds*)
Could you loosen these? I haven't got any
circulation. My legs are asleep. My arms—

145

PUNISHER

Really?

TERRORIST

You're not a torturer, are you? You seem
civilized.

PUNISHER: (*laughs*)

Seem civilized. <u>You</u> seem civilized—what-
ever that can mean. But it's a good question.
I've asked myself that question. I think the
answer is that I'm about to become a deep
torturer.

TERRORIST

Then why did you give me the aspirin and the
drink? That's not the sort of thing a torturer
does. That's the act of a humanist.

PUNISHER

Oh . . . I wanted your full attention. You can't
pay any attention to me when you're suffering
in the throes of a headache.

TERRORIST

(*shakes his head*)

I don't understand you, I admit it. Deep
torturer! What does that mean?

PUNISHER

It means redeemer. It means that I'm not out
to punish your body.

TERRORIST

Then loosen these bonds.

PUNISHER

Perhaps.

TERRORIST

What do you mean, deep torturer?

PUNISHER

Redeemer, redeemer! I mean that I've thought
and thought about it. I mean . . .
    (*picks up automatic*)
look at the weapons you choose.

TERRORIST

    (*looking at the automatic*)
My pistol?

PUNISHER

Yes. Look at it. Sprays venom. Now look at
this.
    (*hefts his revolver, aims at*
    TERRORIST's *head*)
One shot.
    (*cocks revolver*)

TERRORIST
(*nervous but trying to remain calm*)
You don't mean to kill me.

PUNISHER
No.
(*holding the revolver in place*)
I could hit you between the eyes at the
distance of a city block.

TERRORIST
Meaning . . .?

PUNISHER
Meaning that I don't spray venom like a
spitting reptile. Like a cold-blooded snake.
Meaning that I'm selective. I choose my
victim.
(*snaps the trigger, quickly*)

TERRORIST
(*visibly shaken*)
You sonofabitch!

PUNISHER
(*rests revolver in his lap, shakes head*)
That—was a wanton act. That—was an act of
torture.
(*looks at* TERRORIST)

PUNISHER (*Cont'd*)
You see, I can tell the difference. I've still got
enough humanity to possess a conscience. I
know that what I just did was wrong.
>（*gets up, paces, revolver dangling
>from hand*）

Oh, I've thought about it for a long time.
>（*as if to himself*）

No, I'm just a simple soldier. At first it was
vengeance. But I cooled off. I thought about
it.
>（*looks at* TERRORIST *while pacing
>in front of him*）

I asked myself what kind of human being . . .
no, sub-human . . . could send letters through
the mail to blow off the fingers of secretaries.
>（*he looks up*）

I have access to files. I know your ilk. I know
you, particularly. You're . . . your family's
quite wealthy.
>（*stops pacing before* TERRORIST,
>*looks at him*）

You, dear boy, area spoiled brat.
>（*passes on, pacing*）

TERRORIST
>（*defending himself, almost as if to
>himself*）

I have a cause.

PUNISHER
(*whirls about, angry*)
You have a vanity!
(*more calmly*)
You have an arrogance.
(*faces* TERRORIST *again*)
You have a will to be constrained, by no political system.
(*paces again, turns back to*
TERRORIST)
If you got what you want, it would pall
immediately. Immediately, you'd want
something else. Then and there. What you
want is . . . is . . .
(*whirls to face* TERRORIST)
obedience!

TERRORIST
I want to help in the struggle against fascism!

PUNISHER
(*this time whirling upstage,*
PUNISHER *simply laughs, waves his*
hands, revolver still dangling)
But, my boy, you <u>are</u> a fascist!
(*walks downstage*)
You see, every baby is born a fascist. Every
baby wants what it wants when it wants it.
And this is as it should be. And every baby
will use every means at its disposal to get what

PUNISHER (*Cont'd*)

it wants. And what parent, late at night, has
not been the victim of a torturing baby, who
uses its shrill cry to make you move and move
quick. Babies are fascists—one in the same.
Like physical torture. And you, my boy, have
simply never grown up. You see, you're that
thing most to be feared . . . . A willful child
with a machine gun.

     (*picks up the automatic*)

You see?

     (*holding it under* TERRORIST's *nose.*
     Puts it back on desk and holds up his
     own revolver)

A man's weapon. The weapon of a skillful,
selective, mature human being.

TERRORIST

You're as crazy as they come.

PUNISHER (*shrugs*)

Admittedly. As I told you, I'm not a philosopher. I'm a soldier.

TERRORIST

Not a torturer, or so you say. Loosen these
ropes.

PUNISHER

Why not?

*(Takes knife from pocket. Digs
roughly under ropes. Cuts them.
TERRORIST lunges at PUNISHER.
PUNISHER steps back. TERRORIST
falls, cannot move. Rubs legs.)*

TERRORIST

Oh, God, I'm like putty.

PUNISHER

*(Sits on desk. Aims revolver at
TERRORIST)*
Oh, you're a helpless victim.

TERRORIST

Not so helpless in a few minutes. Let me get
my circulation back.

PUNISHER

The thing is, you're like an infant. During the
course of growing up, you never acquired a
conscience. No, you've been deprived. When
you commit an act of terrorism, apparently it
doesn't trouble you that you've made handless
or legless or sightless, or lifeless, another
human being.

TERRORIST

What about you? You're a bloody soldier.

TERRORIST (*Cont'd*)
You've wounded people. Killed them
probably.

PUNISHER
Yes. Troublesome, isn't it? I've thought
about it. As I was preparing for this I thought
a good deal about it. The only thing I can
come up with is the fact of randomness.

TERRORIST
What about your bloody bombs? What about
Dresden? Hiroshima? Nagasaki? London?
Bunch of a sonofabitching soldiers doing that
wasn't it? There were innocents in those
cities, weren't there?

PUNISHER
Oh, God.

TERRORIST
Don't call him in on it now.
(*sits up, rubs arms*)

PUNISHER
Yes. That's a terrible question.

TERRORIST
Nothing selective there, eh?

PUNISHER

Yes. It amounts to the question—don't you think?—of whether we're all mad, all sane, and, therefore, evil, and that, then, there must be good, too. Doesn't it amount to that?

TERRORIST

(*rubs arms again*)
Look, you bastard, I'm no bloody philosopher either!

PUNISHER

(*waves revolver*)
Crawl back, over there.
(TERRORIST *moves back. Starts*
to get up. PUNISHER *points revolver.*)
Stay on the floor. Back.
(TERRORIST *struggles back.*)
Maybe the answer is that evil is who initiates—who starts the thing.

TERRORIST

To hear you talk, babies start it.

PUNISHER

No. I've got to stay with my point. My only sanity is my point.

TERRORIST

Which is?

PUNISHER

That people have to suffer for the crimes they
commit . . . for the evil they do. That they
can't suffer unless they have a conscience.
That that's what I mean by deep torture. I
think the difference between you and me is
that I have a conscience. It does seem
different to me, that when a man tries to kill
me, in defending myself, I kill him, than if I
were the one who decided to do the killing
first. That does seem different to me. The
secretary didn't try to kill you.

TERRORIST

I didn't try to kill her, either. I didn't know
she existed.

PUNISHER

No, you see, there's the point. You just meant
to inflict pain, death, upon someone, anyone.
Yes.
          (*points revolver like a finger*)
Yes. That's the point. You were the initiator.

TERRORIST

So I'm the bloke without the conscience, is
that it?

PUNISHER

That's it.

155

TERRORIST

Oh, I get your point, all right. It doesn't make
a hellova lot of sense. My point is that we're
in a war here—

PUNISHER

(*raises revolver to indicate silence*)
No. You see, you are permanently out of the
war. You may get your circulation back, but
you're not going back into circulation. No,
not you.

TERRORIST

You mean you're going to hold me prisoner?
You said before that you didn't intend to kill
me.

PUNISHER

I don't. That's why I'm going to have to be
very careful.

TERRORIST

You do intend to torture me, then.

PUNISHER

I'm going to have to inflict pain. But I would
do what I intend to do without inflicting pain
if I could.

TERRORIST
(*frightened, confused*)
Damn you! What is it you intend to do?

PUNISHER
When you leave here, and you will leave, you
will be a changed man. You will begin a
lifelong process of learning remorse. I'm
going to make you grow up, laddie buck.
You're going to learn what it is really like to
share this planet with other members of your
species. In your mind, which will gradually
develop a heart,
(*throws out a hand*)
a conscience, you will be deeply tortured for
the rest of your life. Because you have never
understood what it is to see yourself in another
being—sympathy—empathy. You've been
locked in a cell all your life, laddie. But I'm
going to lock you in so tight and for so long
that you'll scream silence night and day for the
word of another human being. For the sight of
a face. For the grace to move with another in
a dance.

TERRORIST
What in hell are you going to do?

PUNISHER
I've thought about it for a long time, laddie.

PUNISHER (*Cont'd*)

I'm going to lock you in your body. All by
yourself.

TERRORIST (*terrified*)

What? What? What?

PUNISHER

I'm going to cut your tongue out, so that
you'll never be able but to vomit sound. I'm
going to hold this pistol next to your eardrums
and fire it, so that you'll never hear the sound
of a voice again. I'm going to use my thumbs
on your eyes. I'm going to castrate you. And
I'm going to break your elbows and knees, and
I'm going to see to it that you live. And for
the rest of your days your punishment will be–
      (*throws out a hand*)
isolation.

TERRORIST

And you, you bastard! You call yourself a
man of conscience?

PUNISHER

Oh, I know, I know. I've thought about it a
great deal. I've thought it all out for a long,
long time.

TERRORIST
(*with a little bravado*)
You can't do it!
(*more bravado*)
You haven't got it in you, to do a thing like
that. You're just trying to frighten me.

PUNISHER
(*looks at* TERRORIST, *no bluffs*)
Yes. I can do it.
(*pauses, thinking*)
But, at first, I thought I couldn't do it unless—

TERRORIST
Unless?

PUNISHER
Unless, after I'd done it, I killed myself.

TERRORIST
My God, you do mean it, don't you?

PUNISHER
(*looking at* TERRORIST)
Yes, I mean it.
(*as if thinking to himself, almost
dreamlike*)
But then I thought . . . then I thought that
would be cheating.

TERRORIST
Cheating what? God?

PUNISHER
No. Myself. My conscience. You see, if I
want you to suffer remorse, then I have no
right to escape it. That's what I meant when I
said earlier that in condemning you, in . . .
        (*looking for the word*)
acting as your therapist, in awarding you the
gift of a conscience . . . well,
        (*throws out hands*)
how could I run out on my own?
        (TERRORIST *in desperation, leaps at*
        PUNISHER. *In reflex,* PUNISHER
        fires, hitting TERRORIST *between the*
        eyes. TERRORIST *falls to floor.*)
No. Oh, no, no, no.
        (standing over TERRORIST)
Oh, God! Oh God!

(CURTAIN)

MARIJUANA AT MONTECELLO

<u>Cast of Characters</u>

Tour Guide: Voice off-stage

<u>Thomas Jefferson</u>:   Director's choice.

<u>Sally Hemmings</u>:   Director's choice.

<u>Scene</u>

Library/study at Monticello.

<u>Time</u>

Imaginary present.

SETTING: THOMAS JEFFERSON's
                  empty study at Monticello.

AT RISE: We hear low, indistinguish-
                  able voices off stage.
                  Sounds of people milling
                  about.

TOUR GUIDE
(*voice-over*)

Stay together, please. Many believe Thomas
Jefferson to have been the greatest of the
Founding Fathers. A liberal in the classic, not
the modern sense, he did not believe in big
government. That government is best, he
wrote, that governs least. In fact, he considered government service not as a career at
all, but as a duty, in the sense that the
legendary Cincinnatus of Rome considered it.
You will remember that Cincinnatus left his
farms to save Rome and returned to them as
soon as possible after the crisis. Jefferson did
not even state that he had been President of the
United States on his gravestone, nor that he,
along with James Madison—and with Ben
Franklin's input—wrote the Constitution of
the United States. He was proudest of the fact

TOUR GUIDE (*Cont'd*)
that he founded the University of Virginia. A
man with a profoundly enquiring mind, he
considered his work in education to be his
truest legacy. An architect, lawyer, writer,
farmer, inventor—his accomplishments are
numerous, outside the field of politics.
Nothing was lost on him. A gourmand, he did
not consider it to be a minor point that he
brought the French fried potato back from
France to his homeland. He was a connoisseur
of wines. A self-taught chef. Truly, a man for
all seasons. As tall as Lincoln, he was a handsome, red-headed man built like an athlete.
Now, follow me. I'm going to take you into
his study—

JEFFERSON
(*Enters, wearing work clothes,
smudged on clothing and face with dirt,
sweating. He goes to bookcase and
searches for something. Mutters to
himself.*)
Cannabis. Cannabis.
(*There is a soft knock on the door.
SALLY HEMINGS steps in.*)

SALLY
Am I disturbing you?

JEFFERSON

No, no, my dear.
> (*He extends his hands to her and she
> crosses to him. They clasp hands and
> then he takes her in his arms and
> kisses her, a long, passionate kiss. He
> releases her, feigning annoyance.*)

Now you've made me forget what I was
looking for, you vixen. Should I pursue you
through the house like a hang-tongued hound?

SALLY

A red bloodhound after a black bunny? You
sweet-assed man, you mastermind, what are
you after? It's not me, when you're onto an
idea.

JEFFERSON

I've been planting an exotic, a plant with
extraordinary properties. It produces a
narcotic affect, quite pleasant, when smoked.
I have reason to believe it could be of
enormous medicinal value. It's called
Cannabis.
> (*continues looking in bookcase*)

SALLY

Pot! You been planting pot?

JEFFERSON

No, no, my silly. I've been planting it on
yonder hill.
            (*pointing out window*)

SALLY

Thomas Jefferson. You mean to say you don't
know?

JEFFERSON

Know what, my dear? What are you on about?

SALLY

Why, you can't plant marijuana on yon hill.
The D.E.A.—

JEFFERSON

The what—who—?

SALLY

The D.E.A., the Drug Enforcement Agency.
They fly helicopters and light planes over here
all the time. They'll spot your pot and raid
Monticello. They break down your door and
make you lie facedown on the floor and
handcuff you from behind and drag you off,
you big fool!

JEFFERSON

These helicopters—sun-drawn seeds? You've

JEFFERSON (*Cont'd*)
become quite the scientist. Exceeded the
teacher, for I must admit I have not heard of
them before. What books are you reading?

SALLY
Never mind that, Tom. The D.E.A.'ll—

JEFFERSON
Are they some secret band of terrorist sent by
the mad old king? Are the English still after
revenge for the Revolution? We have many
friends in Parliament, but there are always
diehards. Should we raise an armed militia?
It was for such types, and others—primarily,
for those in the government of the United
States who would attempt to reduce the dream
of freedom that is America, that I and the
others made certain that the citizen could
retain his weapons of defense. I feared a
tyrannical taxation, which is the first tool of
tyrants in their attempt to subjugate their
subjects. Next is open force. (*He ponders*)
So, the Brits are at it again. Call out the
militia!

SALLY
No, Tom, not the Brits. Parliament doesn't
pay any heed to the mad old king anymore.

JEFFERSON

Who, then? And why should this D.E.A.—did
you call them?—why should they care what I
do? What possible difference can it make to
anyone, that I am experimenting with
Cannabis? I have experimented with things all
my life. It is the nature of the mind to explore.
How is it any of their affair?

SALLY

They are a government agency, Tom.

JEFFERSON

Is this a nightmare? Are you telling me that
the government of the United States of
America would have anything to do with what
a citizen does on his own land and in the
privacy of his home, barring, of course, some
criminal activity?

SALLY

But growing marijuana _is_ a criminal activity.

JEFFERSON

How, confound it! It is an interest of mine,
and it has become a pleasure, like my wines,
like my French fried potatoes. What in
heaven's name are you on about?

SALLY

They have made a law against it.

JEFFERSON

Why that would be exactly like making a law against opium. Why would anyone do that?

SALLY

There is a law against opium—the same law.

JEFFERSON

Opium is against the law? Why? It has marvelous properties.

SALLY

They don't want people to use drugs.

JEFFERSON

Who are <u>they</u>, that they should tell the people what to do? Perhaps it's time for another revolution. Next you'll be telling me there's a law against wine, the first miracle of Christ.

SALLY

There will be—between Nineteen-Nineteen and Nineteen Thirty-three. It will be called Prohibition.

JEFFERSON (*astounded*)

Prohibition! To prohibit? The United States

JEFFERSON (*Cont'd*)
Government is in the business of prohibiting
people from ingesting wine and good stout and
bourbon whiskey and of all things, opium.
Why?

SALLY
It's not good for us.

JEFFERSON
Who are they to say what is and is not good
for anyone?   The people decide that,
individually. There is nothing malum in se,
evil in itself, about any intoxicant. Life is
difficult, one escapes it from time to time. It is
perfectly normal. One does it in reading a
book, watching a play, in conversation over
wine, in watching a sunset. Prohibition? That
is merely malum prohibitum, an evil because it
is called one. And by whom? Let him who
does not enjoy wine do what he does enjoy. I
enjoy wine. What is it to him?
> (*goes to a sideboard and pours
> himself a drink, drinks it, then pours
> both of them a drink and hands one to
> her.*)
I must admit to shock. This has happened
since my retirement?

SALLY

This and much more since you set me free.

JEFFERSON

I had not the power to set anyone free, my
love. There is another example of the evil of
law, what tyranny it becomes when unre-
strained. How people give their freedom away
for a false safety. Life is not a thing to feel
safe in.

SALLY

A security blanket.

JEFFERSON

Yes, yes, that's very good. Yes, life is not a
security blanket to feel safe in, it is a thrilling
adventure, dangerous and doomed, but it
offers the opportunity, once in the universe of
eternity, to test one's metal, to see if the
stardust can hold its own.

SALLY

You're wonderful with words, Tom. But you
must go out and deracinate that pot.

JEFFERSON

Never! I stand on my Constitutional rights.
After all, I wrote them. This government has
its priorities misplaced. Every person has as

JEFFERSON (*Cont'd*)

much right to do as he or she desires to do as
does the government, which is only another
group of persons, somewhat less talented than
the average artist or scientist, mostly middle-
brow lawyers. The government is here to see
that we do not hurt one another and are not
hurt from the outside. We are here to see to it
that the government doesn't hurt us. Have you
not heard me say, my dear, that when the
candidates tell you they have a plan, you
should tell them that you already have a plan.
It's called the Constitution of the United States
of America, and proceed to inform them that
they are not James Madison, et alia. The
purpose of the Constitution is well known.
It's purpose is to keep out subsequent plans by
politicians, including candidates. Its purpose
is to make the government leave the citizen
alone. This is called freedom and is highly
valued by all enslaved peoples, though not so
highly valued as it ought to be by those
possessed of it. Freedom allows for invention,
invention creates wealth, wealth is a syrup one
pours into pies, causing them to expand their
crusts, crack, and ooze rich juices that drip . . .
all over the place!

SALLY

That's all very well, Tom, but, as to the drugs,

SALLY (*Cont'd*)
they would say that they cause violence.

JEFFERSON
How? Oh, I've been in a taphouse brawl or
two. I might not look it today, but I was quite
accomplished in the art of fisticuffs when in
my youth.

SALLY
I love your muscles, my dear. No, but that
isn't what they mean. There are those who
shoot each other over the drugs. Dealers and
the like.

TOUR GUIDE
(*voice-over*)
Right this way, now—into the garden.

SALLY
They'll see the pot out there.

JEFFERSON
Let them. I told you, my dearest, I planted the
cannabis in the ground, not in a pot. Why do
you keep insisting—?

SALLY
Tom, pour me another drink, please. I need
one.

JEFFERSON

It's particularly good Amontillado. (*pouring*)
We had a boy at the University of Virginia, I
heard, an extremely intelligent chap name of
Edgar Poe, who wrote a wonderful tale called
the Cask of Amontillado. I enjoyed it
immensely.

(*handing her a glass*)

Do you know, speaking of intoxicants, this
young Poe was said to have experimented with
all manner of them. I was so interested. I
wanted to have him come for a visit but I was
never able to locate him. Bit of a bounder, I'm
told, but I can't help think that anyone who
can write like that must have the stuff.
Dropped out, unfortunately, after only a year.
Money problems, gambling, or something.

SALLY

My dearest, you don't seem to understand the
danger you're in. The D.E.A. plays rough.

JEFFERSON

Rougher than the Brits? I doubt it. And we
sent Cornwallis on his way. Now, there again,
is an example of what I mean. Taxation, the
tool of tyranny!

SALLY

That's how they pay the D.E.A.

174

JEFFERSON
What? You mean with <u>our</u> taxes? I remember old Ben Franklin used to say, there are only two certainties in life, death and taxes. I always liked that one. But how do they extract such taxes?

SALLY
From income.

JEFFERSON
Tyranny, tyranny, tyranny, and the end of wealth. For a man of spirit will not work for under fifty percent of his labor's worth.

SALLY
Poor Tom, you ain't seen nothing yet!

JEFFERSON
No, no. "Haven't" and "Anything."

SALLY
I know, precious baby, I know.

TOUR GUIDE
(*voice-over*)
Someone has planted marijuana in President Jefferson's garden. Marijuana at Monticello, can you imagine? But wait! What's that? There are Apache helicopters overhead. You

TOUR GUIDE (*Cont'd*)
can see the rockets and the machine guns.
They are an American fleet. I can see the flag-
emblem of the United States of America—
and, something else—what is it?—D.E.A. Oh
my God, people, run for your lives!

SALLY
Tom, Monticello is being stormed. Where can
we hide?

JEFFERSON
Hide, nothing! Hand me my long-rifle. I'll
take my stand for liberty!

(CURTAIN)